Voice from the Mountain

Voice from the Mountain

New Life for the Old Law

edited by
Philip Jefferson

Anglican Book Centre
Toronto, Canada

© Copyright 1982
by Anglican Book Centre
Published by
Anglican Book Centre
600 Jarvis Street
Toronto, Ontario
Canada M4Y 2J6

Printed in Canada
ISBN 919030-77-7

Cover design by
Saskia Walther

Cover photo courtesy of
Miller Services

Contents

Contributors

John Bothwell, bishop of the Diocese of Niagara, centred in Hamilton, Ontario, is active in the Regional Social Planning Council, and national and provincial church projects. Married with five grown children, he is an advocate of orthodox faith, liberally interpreted, in an open Christian church community.

Sister Constance, S.S.J.D. is a member of the Society of St John the Divine. Now in her seventies, she has recently studied extensively in the field of gerontology, an area in which she also does much of her ministry.

Phyllis Creighton, an editor for *The Dictionary of Canadian Biography* of the University of Toronto Press, has written *Artificial Insemination by Donor* and edited *Abortion: An Issue for Conscience*. An active member of St Philip the Apostle Church in Toronto, she is married to Philip W. Creighton and is the mother of four children.

Gordon Fairweather is the first Canadian Human Rights Commissioner, an office he assumed in 1977. From 1952–1962 he served in the New Brunswick legislature, and then for 15 years he was the Member of Parliament for Fundy-Royal.

Ebert Hobbs is the director of Anglicans in Mission, the three year project of the Anglican Church. He has held positions with the National Council of Churches and the Episcopal Diocese of Ohio, and has prepared The Covenant Plan stewardship program.

Philip Jefferson, rector of St James' Parish, Dundas, Ontario, was formerly the editorial secretary of the Department of Religious Education of the Anglican Church. The author of numerous articles on Christian education, he was the editor of *The Church in the Sixties* and of Parish Education Program teaching materials.

Barbara J. Ball Liotscos is priest assistant at St Faith's Anglican Church in Vancouver, B.C., having earned her B.A. in English and Psychology at Queens' University, Kingston, and her M. Div. at the Vancouver School of Theology. She is married with one daughter.

James Reed, an Anglican priest, is associate professor of Pastoral Psychology and Counselling at Trinity College and the Toronto School of Theology. He is a psychotherapist in private practice for individuals, families, and married couples, and a member of the executive of the International Committee of Pastoral Care and Counselling.

Anthony M. Waterman is a graduate of Cambridge who moved to St John's College, Winnipeg to study theology and teach economics and political science. He was the principal author of *Poverty in Canada: A Christian Perspective*, and is now working on a study of Christian political economy.

James Wilkes, a psychiatrist with theological background, is on the staff of the Scarborough Centenary Hospital in Toronto and is a consultant to several community agencies. Wilkes, who served as a missionary to India early in his medical career, is an honorary lecturer in the Department of Psychiatry at the University of Toronto and lectures widely on the subject of religion and mental health. He is also the author of *The Gift of Courage*.

Preface

The purpose of this book is to assist lay people and clergy to think about the world today in the light of our traditions, and to see some directions for the future.

In the Sermon on the Mount, Jesus helped his audience see the Ten Commandments in terms that were relevant for their day. Although this book does not claim to be a new Sermon on the Mount, it attempts to do a similar task. Ten of the "followers in the Way" of the 1980s have undertaken to look at the Decalogue, and to share their thoughts on what the Law of Moses says to us now.

Generally the writers have had to be selective in their focus on the commandments, but the richness of the Law means that other viewpoints are very possible. If these chapters encourage further explorations by the reader, that is all to the good. In this book, we have tried to see connections with popular ideologies, family life, world issues, and personal moral choices, as well as relationships with the economic, political, liturgical, biblical, and educational spheres of our existence. If we are not exhaustive in our survey, we are at least diverse!

Also, due to space limitations, the authors have not included extensive footnotes for references. They would, however, be happy to respond to any written inquiries about sources or further reading.

Someone estimated that we have 35 million laws trying to enforce the Ten Commandments. Exaggerated or not, there is truth in the statement. To live with these laws, to interpret them, to re-shape and change them with time, we must consider their roots in the divine law of God. As we live in the 1980s, the vast changes we continue to experience must be related to these roots.

In an age when we are rediscovering some of the traditional values of worship and faith, and expressing them in new ways, I hope this book will make a contribution to our continuing journey.

Philip Jefferson

The Other Gods of the Eighties

James Wilkes

1 Thou shalt have none other gods but me

On the ceiling of the Sistine Chapel, Michelangelo has painted God and Adam in a relationship of intimacy. They are face to face, looking each other straight in the eye, with their hands stretched out so that they can touch. Michelangelo has used the story of Adam and Eve to capture and present visually the heart of the Judeo-Christian understanding of man, which is that he was made for relationship with God. The actual story from Genesis depicts Adam and Eve in such a close relationship with God that they do not even question it. They walk naked before God, and because they have no need to know their nakedness, they do not.

The story is, however, also a story about the breaking of relationship. It is the beguiling serpent who suggests that the forbidden fruit be eaten. The serpent is able to instil the idea that it is possible to act other than in a way God wants; at this point the relationship with God is open to question. Until this point, the rule was Adam and Eve's orientation — they knew no other. The genius of the story of Adam and Eve is to point out the truth that when man entertains the thought that his orientation can somehow be other than God, he is at once self-oriented, and so dis-oriented. The story highlights Adam and Eve's disorientation by having them know that they are naked. They ate of the tree and, thereby, broke their relationship with God, and now in their disorientation they must cover themselves. From a relationship of oneness with God they have moved to separateness and otherness, and so they must protect themselves.

Relationship is a central theme in Judeo-Christian theology. The God of Judeo-Christian tradition is a God of relationship. He is not remote, but present and caring about human history. The Hebrew people, through their experience in Egypt, gradually developed an understanding of God that was deeper and richer than those of other nations and tribes of the time. Through historical encounter with their Egyptian captors, they gained an understanding that God was with them. More than that, they also wove into this historical reality the ancient stories of Abraham, Isaac, and Jacob, the stories of covenant — the stories that spoke of God taking care of them and always being faithful to them.

After the Exodus, when the people were having difficulties in the wilderness, they lost faith in God, and in their disorientation they began to worship other gods. Idolatry takes place in the disorientation that follows the breaking of covenant. But at Sinai God reaffirmed his faithfulness through Moses by providing the law.

Thou shalt have none other Gods but me. This first commandment is not only an order to man, it is more, much more — it is a gift. It offers the gift of relationship with God; it offers orientation. In a sense, it is preposterous to think of any other God because all other gods would be illusions. There is only one Almighty God. What this commandment does is to recognize that humanity can be disoriented and lost in illusion, and it commands the people to stay with God. In disorientation people cannot find a center — they remain eccentric and persue goals that are illusory, empty, dangerous, and self destructive. Having lost orientation, men and women are adrift and vulnerable. Into this drifting, eccentric, disoriented state comes the anchoring, centering, orienting clear thrust of truth — Thou shalt have none other Gods but me. For humankind this is not only a command but an opportunity!

The other gods of today, as other gods always have, will disappear in the light of this first commandment. The gods of today are no different than those of the past. They have been made in order to fill the gaps of emptiness, loneliness, and meaninglessness that permeate human lives. Illusory gods fill the gaps that form as people separate themselves from God. They grow out of disorientation, and they contribute to it. Anything becomes deified when it is sought as an end in itself. There is only one end to be sought, and that is relationship with God and, therefore, with creation as it is centered in him. Thou shalt have none other gods but me. The question for people is whether to obey the commandment and remain in covenant with God, or to put faith in the false gods of their own making.

Me-ism

One of the most powerful, persuasive, and dangerous false gods of today is the god Me-ism. Me-ism is the conviction that I own the life I live — that, in an ultimate sense, the life I live is mine. Me-ism — the confusion that I am life or life is me — is appropriately worded. I-ism would indicate some kind of subjective identity, but when a person is firmly in the embrace of Me-ism, there is no subject left — only object!

I lose my life when I take it to make it mine. Life must never become a possession; rather it must remain the gift that it is. Certainly the scriptures are quite clear about this — the self satisfied man who has it all made, and now all he need do is eat, drink, and be merry, is told that he is a fool.[1]

The ground of reality is covenant — relationship with God and with others. Me-ism presses a person to isolation and aloneness. The spirit of the god Me-ism is summed up well in the so-called prayer. "I do my thing, and you do your thing. I am not in this world to live up to your expectation, and you are not in this world to live up to mine. You are you and I am I, and if by chance we happen to find each other, it's beautiful."[2] Don't worry about commitment, don't worry about anyone else, you are you and I am I.

A frequent experience of those who are dying of incurable illness is the liberating feeling they obtain when Me-ism is exposed for what it is. When they give up the idea that they must control their life, they are then free to accept their life as a gift. They are able to leave their petulance and anger over not living as long as they expected, and although saddened, they become free to accept the gift that their life has been and still is.

The god Me-ism is destructive to mental health, particularly in the areas where power and prestige are sought for the sake of self. The burden that people inflict on themselves in order to be perfect, in order to be the best, can destroy themselves and others. The unhappy business man scarcely seen by his family and grouchy when he is, who is drinking more than he should, and who always seems dissatisfied, worships Me-ism. The student who gets no pleasure from her learning because she is afraid her grades might slip and she won't stand at the top of the class, worships the same god. The need to be number one is certainly prevalent in our society where sports fans ecstatically wave with pointed finger yelling, "We are number one." This is harmless enough perhaps when it stops at the sports stadium, but there is evidence that the need to be number one has far more sinister expressions.

The moving music of Elgar's "Pomp and Circumstance" carries the lines, "God, who made us mighty, make us mightier yet." When one thinks of mightyness, one rarely thinks of whom one is to be mightier than. Does one country deserve to be mightier than another because of some special merit? Perhaps it is better and should stay mightier until the other improves! Should one be mightier than another forever? When people talk about being number one, what thoughts have they about number two, number ten, number one hundred? The God of Abraham, Isaac, and Jacob in the person of the Christ spoke about being among people as slaves — what number does the slave get?

The sinister and disorienting effect of Me-ism is illustrated by comparing two events. The first event was witnessed by many people one evening at a concert hall. The pianist Vladimir Horowitz had just completed a brilliant and moving execution of his skill. For an hour and a half he had played and the audience had listened, and with many of them he had been one. At the end of the performance he left his piano and stood amid the applause; then slowly, with pointed finger, like Michelangelo's fresco, he reached out to the audience gently swinging his arm back and forth across the auditorium up even to the reaches of the very top balcony. He touched everyone there and gave them life! His great musical ability was not claimed by the god Me-ism, but was given with joy and delight to the people. The gift of his ability was shared in relationship with others.

The second event was witnessed by nobody. That same evening another pair of hands were at work, but these hands were driven by a different purpose. These fingers were fashioning the means of the owner's death. No pretty music here. This bright, able, kind young woman could no longer tolerate her inadequacy. For her, life no longer seemed to hold any value; she was alone, and she deliberately and skilfully killed herself. The audience she was striving to impress was never there. Her disorientation had reached the point where she was demanding more and more of herself, and bright and talented as she was, she still couldn't do the impossible. She saw herself as the only means of improving things, but her expectations for herself were so great that they couldn't be met. It all became hopeless and futile. Her life can be laid as victim at the altar of the god Me-ism.

The victims of Me-ism are not only individuals. Institutions can in a corporate sense become self-oriented and, therefore, disoriented. This is no less true for the Church which, when it closes its eyes and ears to the world, becomes caught up in talking to itself and thinking only about itself. The desire to meet people's demands for security, certitude, and perfection can close the Church to the struggles and ambiguities of the world. From the healthy position of being a people journeying in faith, the church can become stationary and turned into pursuits of its own control and domination over people's lives. Carl Jung spoke of this in his last publication, stating that "the Christian puts the Church and his Bible between himself and his unconscious." For Jung it was necessary for people to be open to the unconscious in order to receive psychological nourishment, energy, and imagination, and so to be protected from the self destruction that occurs and will continue to occur, perhaps in increasingly horrific fashion, if the unconscious is denied and left to its own devices. Any move by the church to establish a permanent and safe retrenchment into certainty of doctrine or spirituality is to deny the unconscious and to deny the truth in life itself. Such a move to safety opens mankind to danger. The Church has always to be willing to let go the safety and imprisonment of its Egypts and to journey into the wilderness. In making the journey, the first thing to be left behind must be the god Me-ism.

The disorienting effect of the god of Me-ism can in turn promote the growth of other gods. Four of them are particularly significant in our age — energy, technology, experience, and passivity.

Energy

Energy and power are necessary for things to happen — necessary for life itself. From the blink of an eye to the formation of the universe, nothing happens without energy and power. Power itself is necessary to sustain creation. So, like all of his creation, God may look upon power and see that it is good. It is never evil in itself, but it becomes so when it is deified, when it is sought as an end in itself. Energy then can become a god in its own right.

Once one is firmly under the influence of the god of energy, he or she feels free to use it in any way deemed fit. Take a spin in the car, put in more air conditioners, turn up the furnace; it matters not, as long as nobody gets hurt! The energy crisis is beginning to sensitize people to the fact that non-renewable sources of energy are fast depleting, and that the unlimited use of energy has led humanity to the brink of the abyss. Without energy the Western economy will collapse, and the way will be paved for political and social upheaval on a global scale. The retreat from the abyss cannot even begin until the god of energy is renounced and the people struggle towards a just, sustainable, and participatory policy in their handling of it.

Technology

The god of energy has its twin in the god of technology. The major theme of this god is "every problem has a solution." This is shown in its most ludicrous form when technology renders life itself into a series of problems so that all that is left is to find the solutions. Find the appropriate expert, and one's problems disappear. Take a complicated and ambiguous human situation, put it into technological language, turn the crank, and presto — here is the solution! No account is taken of the human and ecological context, and technology becomes an end in itself.

Humanity is from *humus*, the earth. Humility is not an affliction but an orientation! Yet one great illusion of technology is that as we expand our limits we can somehow transcend ourselves. But our nature can not change through technological advance. The degree to which the god of technology can lead to disorientation is illustrated in this statement from a proponent of a new technological age — "We humans do not want to be God or play God. We aspire to much more. God was a cruel concept, vengeful and wrathful, destructive. We humans want to evolve beyond God."[3]

In the middle of the twentieth century there was the feeling not that we would evolve beyond God but, at least, that there was no obstacle that science could not eventually overcome. The application of science through technology would make life safe and happy for all.

Technology was to be the panacea for mankind and, indeed, technology has brought benefits to mankind in, for example, medical science, communication, and transportation. However, technology seems to have outstripped our capacity to handle it. Nuclear technology has given the atom bombs; biological technology has opened fearsome possibilities in the field of genetic engineering. The ravages to the world's ecology, the ugly realities of pollution, the danger of acid rain, and the misuse of technology in the third world hardly attest to technology being a panacea. Our future now seems inextricably linked to technology, and romantic notions of a radical getting back to nature, even if this were possible, overlook the economic and political repercussions of any drastic abandoning of technology. Technology will continue to develop, but we can no longer look to it as a means of our freedom from pain, disease, or fear. The god of technology must be renounced so that technology can be taken up with hands that love and care for other human beings, and for those yet to be born.

Experience

There is another god which has considerable popular appeal. When a person feels that he or she is the center of reality, when life is seen as a possession, when self is put before relationship, then one is easily led to worship the god of experience. Those who worship the god of experience think that experience itself is the main objective in life. This idea has current appeal in many so called therapies, guided only by the thought that experience is good for us. People are encouraged to get in touch with themselves, to learn about themselves in new and novel surroundings. There seems to be no limit to the kinds of behaviour people can be pushed into — all with the misguided notion that this is good for them. People are encouraged to let go their inhibitions and to do their own thing. The key word in one current popular "therapy" is *experience*, and the main goal of the training is to get the participants to "transform their ability to experience living." Nowhere is there any question of what lies behind any of this. A proponent of this therapy writes, "You are the supreme being. Reality is a reflection of your notions. Totally. Perfectly."[4] This statement shows with remarkable clarity how, when the writer's orientation is lost, his own effort seems to push him deeper into illusion. In this case, his disorientation leads him to the god of experience, and from there he is deluded into thinking that he is God!

The god of experience influences many "therapeutic" endeavors. People can be helped to "learn how to be real." Unfortunately reality never gets defined, but is left in an unspoken useless repetition: "reality is what is experienced." People are helped to develop a variety of content-free expressive and interpersonal skills so that they may be "spontaneous" and thus "experience growth." It doesn't take much to see the serious flaw in such therapy. There is no such thing as behaviour that is free of content — we are more than what we do. We are involved in relationship and we are making history, like it or not! We are disoriented when we think we can engage in content-free or value-free activity.

Separating experience from the rest of life, from such things as value, commitment, and purpose, is destructive to personal growth. When experience is made an end in itself, then there is no need to plan because there will always be something to experience. Without the need to plan, the future is not important, and one does not think much beyond tomorrow. With no context and no purpose, there is little, if anything, to remember. There is no future, no past, and one lives in a time capsule where experience gradually loses its lustre and fades into darkness. In such a state, lying to oneself easily becomes a way of life. The alcoholic will stop drinking tomorrow, the student dropout will soon either find work or return to school, the marriage will be renewed and refreshed if it is "opened" to sexual intimacy with others. Such disorientation grows when we refuse to see that experience is linked to history, because to look at it as separate is idolotrous and, of course, illusory.

Passivity

The god of experience is the power behind another god which is not as well known, apparently innocuous, and sometimes even considered virtuous — the god of passivity. This god holds that taking a stand is to be avoided, that argument is offensive, and that holding convictions is authoritarian. Passivity is not to be confused with kindness, politeness, or gentleness — all of which are important in human relationships. Passivity is, in contrast, destructive to human relationships because it promotes vagueness and indecision, and it does so by undermining all authority. Authority has an integrating quality which is necessary if order is to be maintained, decisions are to be made, and sanity is to prevail. Authority is necessary if anything is to make sense at all. A mind that lacks authority is mad. How does the viewer know that he sees? Where does the person get the authority to say, "I see that . . ." or "I think that . . ."? Without authority how can one come to decision? The god of passivity pushes the mind to mistrust its thoughts, its senses, its feelings. A group without leadership is aimless, a state without authority lives in confusion and anarchy. Jesus, we may remember, was proclaimed as speaking with authority! One cannot have authority and worship the god of passivity.

The health of a community is nurtured when its membership states its opinion. This is true of a marriage, a family, a parish, a nation. When people hold their opinion to themselves, the part of the truth they hold is not shared. We live in a pluralistic society, and in order that it may survive, people must avoid the seduction of passivity. When people stand back, then they abdicate their power and leave the way open to domination by others. Pluralism survives when opinions, people, races, are openly interacting with each other. Intimacy cannot survive without difference. Conflict and argument are necessary if one is to know the distinctiveness of the other's opinion. In relationship it is not argument that matters but the attitude that is taken towards each other. Are people open and listening to each other, or closed and rejecting each other? Love grows ever deeper as one learns of the distinctiveness and the essence of the other. If we are to love one another, we cannot worship the god of passivity.

The First Commandment

The false gods of these times — the gods of Me-ism, energy and technology, experience and passivity, are all destructive of us and the world that we live in. They all, however, are themselves destroyed under the commandment, Thou shalt have none other gods but me. Jesus captured this truth when he was asked by a scribe, "Which commandment is first of all?" Jesus answered, "The first is, 'Hear, O Israel: the Lord our God is the only Lord; love the Lord your God with all your heart, with all your soul, with all your mind, and with all your strength'. The second is this, 'Love your neighbour as yourself'."[5]

It was Jesus who could look through the apparent harshness of that first commandment and remind us of the love that was in the authority. For Jesus, love is the means of obedience and, therefore, of orientation. If God is truly loved, then one would not act to break any of the other commandments. This is picked up in the second part of what Jesus said: "Love thy neighbour as thyself." If we have no other gods but the God of Abraham, Isaac, and Jacob — the God that was fully revealed in Jesus the Christ — then we will see our lives as gifts to be given in relationship to others, then we will use power and energy to build relationships, then we will use technology to facilitate the building, then will our experience be rich and illuminating, and then we can with passion love our God, our neighbour, and ourselves. We will be able to face one another, and look one another straight in the eye, and with our hands we can reach out and touch one another. We will be in loving relationship, not of innocence, but of knowledge. Thou shalt have none other gods but me!

Notes

1 Luke 12:20.

2 Frederick S. Perls; from poster catalogue no. 320, Western Graphics Corporation, Eugene, Oregon.

3 F.M. Estfiandry; quoted by Victor Ferkiss in "Technology and Culture," *Cross Currents* Vol. 30, No. 1, p. 19.

4 Carl Frederick, *est* — *Playing the Game the New Way*, Delta paperback, 1976 p. 171.

5 Mark 12:28b – 31a. Jesus has joined together *Deuteronomy* 6:4 and *Leviticus* 19:18b.

Unto the Third and Fourth Generations

Philip Jefferson

2 Thou shalt not make to thyself any graven image

In many ways, it is difficult to relate the second commandment to ourselves. Partly this is because it conjures up pictures
for us of idols, golden calves, and other carved images. Can we
imagine an Anglican family being tempted to kneel before
them, to touch their heads to the floor, to lift up their hands
and intone prayers to these graven images? We may not know
what all our sins are at any given time, but we are usually certain that breaking the second commandment in this way is not
a daily habit!

And besides, this commandment is one of the longest, with
two paragraphs devoted to it in the Catechism. It was one of
the hardest for a confirmation class to memorize. If we hear it
read in the Eucharist, its significance is often diminished for us
because the celebrant cuts it off at the end of the first
paragraph. It is much easier for us to identify our sinfulness
with false witnessing, stealing, and coveting, than with the
worship of graven images.

Transmitting Values

The truth is that the second commandment touches at the
nerve centre of our lives as believers. It is the future-oriented
command, the one that reminds us of the transmission of
faith. "Visiting the sins" refers to the ways in which values
and faith are passed on from generation to generation. How we
act affects our own children, and helps to shape their beliefs

and values. Their beliefs and values, in turn, influence their own actions, which then affect their children — our grand-children. And so to the third and fourth generation of those who are taught to follow or reject God.

Now that can be a little more devastating! To be reminded that we are influenced by our ancestors, and will in turn shape our descendants, can increase our awareness of the importance of our own faith, not just for our own peace of mind today, but for stability and tranquility, for courage and commitment in years to come, for the generations yet unborn. If we think of our own personal belief and value system, we can perhaps be aware of how we came to be the kind of person we are. It's true that our decisions affect our destiny, but we are also the pro-duct of our forefathers and foremothers. Let me illustrate how I believe this works, by sharing a value from my own back-ground.

I have always been aware that my family tried to be indepen-dent. As long as I can remember, we were encouraged to stand on our own two feet, to tough-it-out ourselves, not to be beholden to others. We had an unwritten caution about the Canadian Establishment whenever it impinged on us. We would certainly never use the influence of our uncle (who was a Canadian senator), or of the Anglican Primate (who was a close college friend of my parents). Our family valued our own bootstraps too highly for any influence peddling! That is appa-rently because my early ancestors were settlers from England and Boston in 1760 on the Nova Scotia farmland vacated by the expulsion of the Acadians. My great-great-great grandfather was a colonel in the militia, a justice of the peace, a member of the Governor's council — respected, responsible, a good citizen. Then, in 1783, the Loyalists flooded into Nova Scotia. The best farms were taken by them, official appointments went to them, they were the new heroes. As times became dif-ficult, many of the pre-Loyalist settlers moved away, discouraged and disheartened by the turn of events. My ancestors stayed, expressing the value of quiet independence, living modestly and spurning the connections which the Loyalists enjoyed. In each succeeding generation, that standard of quiet independence appears again and again. The uncon-scious transmission took place by example. I hold it today, and

I expect that my children and my children's children will hold it also. It's neither a particularly virtuous stance, nor a destructive one. But it certainly is a value for my family!

The second commandment teaches us about the transmission of values, and especially the value of worshipping, loving, and serving God. When we consider the positive aspects of the second commandment, we are aware of the divine blessing that rests on those who love God and keep the commandments. Most parents truly want that which is good for their children. Thus, an awareness of the processes by which we "hand on" to the third and fourth generations the love of God, and the acceptance of God's will, is useful.

Expressing Values

The principal way we communicate what we really believe is through what we do, not what we say. We cannot easily teach good stewardship to our children if we are conspicuous consumers ourselves (see Chapter 10). When we deny our speeding to the police officer, the children in the back seat get a lesson about when to lie. Our worship of God, conducted regularly and devoutly, says much more to our sons and daughters than our sermonettes to them that God must be respected and not cursed. The use of swear words to which we succumb is a subtle contradiction of "thou shalt not take the name of the Lord thy God in vain"! Indeed, Christian educators have been pointing out for years that children's first concepts of what God is like come to them from their parents — how they are cared for, nurtured, protected, disciplined, and forgiven. "In God we trust" can only happen after "in my Mother and Dad I can trust" occurs.

If, therefore, we can see the reality of this transmission of attitudes, beliefs and values by what we do, how can we consciously direct and influence the transmission? In other words, how can we make sure that our children in the next generation are taught what we really want them to learn? Obviously, we need to be aware of what our own values and beliefs really are, where one contradicts another, and how well we live by them ourselves. Therefore, working away at our own Christian faith is important. And the other side of the coin in this process is "intentionality" — intending to communicate what we really believe in our best moments, to those whom we love and about whom we care. This communicating takes place in three different settings over which we have considerable control — our homes, our church schools, and our churches.

Values Expressed at Home

Recently, several of our own grown-up children came home for a dinner party, just after we had moved back into a redecorated dining room. As we chatted about various items of furniture and pieces of china, our daughter-in-law said, "Everything in this home has a story attached to it!" There is a real element of truth for us in that statement. Pictures, books, furniture — many of our household items have been handed on to us. My great aunt left us a large bookcase cabinet in 1954. Grandmother's old steel engraving of 1857, from the country house in Nova Scotia, is on our living room wall. And one wall of the upstairs family room is covered with pictures of ancestors — the family tree.

This sense of ancestry, story, and tradition, has been important for us. In the last twelve years I have collected anecdotes, pictures, clippings, and geneologies to preserve for my children and their sons and daughters. The collection is used to recount tales of citizenship, courage, pioneering, caring, and service. Values of honesty, devotion, and generosity are mingled with tales of humour, tragedy, and mystery. At times, the children groaned at my repetition of the tales once more. But as they connected the stories with the pictures and the furniture, the anecdotes with the characters, they too came to recognize family traits which we believed to be worthwhile, and to develop standards to guide them.

I believe it is necessary and possible to do this in terms of one's biblical ancestry as well. Persons who are serious about transmitting the tradition of Christianity to their children can use the combination of pictures, traditions, practices, and Bible stories. As our Jewish ancestors did, we Christians can retell the events of biblical faith in our homes for our children. When I was young, my mother read stories to my brother, sister, and me at bed time every night. They were books like

Winnie The Pooh, Robinson Crusoe, and *The Bobbsey Twins.*
But on Sunday nights, father would read to us. He would bring
an old and battered copy of Hurlbutt's *Stories of the Bible,* and
read from it. So the biblical tradition took its place with the
secular, but it was somehow special — special day, special
reader. And I grew up knowing the stories of David, Jacob, and
Paul, and quite familiar with the illustrations of events. Dad
never said what they meant, he just told them.

The other element for us at home was the presence of
"church people." The local rector was respected and appre-
ciated, and we invited the curate to come to dinner from time
to time. Mother and Dad referred with appreciation to the
bishop, who was a personal friend of theirs.

These elements, combined and coalesced in our home with
the rest of the family traditions and standards, expressed in
non-verbal ways the values of my parents. Later I found out
that Dad's grandmother had helped teach him by sitting in the
kitchen rocking-chair at the turn of the century, with *her* Bible
in her lap. And on the shelf in my house today is great grandfather's Prayer Book and grandfather's Bible.

Bruno Bettelheim, a child psychologist and author, claims
that the traditional family unit cannot be expected to survive
when most or all of the traditions are gone. Many would con-
cur with that opinion. This is why the development of family
traditions — getting the Christmas tree together, the spring
hike, the summer trip, and so forth — are very important in
creating the sense of stability that is an essential weave in the
fabric of society. When you see a four-year-old take a two-year-
old's hand to bring her with him to the altar rail, that's value
transmitted. When the children share the music of Joe Wise in
some of his marvellous records, that's value transmitted!

We don't all have family furniture going back several generations (some of us wouldn't want it!), but we all have our own
story to share. Collecting the snapshots and making them
accessible to be seen, getting one new ornament for the tree
each Christmas, making a visit regularly or planting a rose
bush each year — you name it for yourself! "Showing mercy
unto the third and fourth generation of them that love me and
keep my commandments" is inextricably interwoven with
this type of reality at home.

The role of the Church School

Two hundred years ago in England, Robert Raikes established the Sunday School. Begun as an attempt to break the failure syndrome of youth in industrialized cities, it developed as an educational arm of the churches. It has had its critics over the years, chiefly because we have expected it to do far more than it is capable of doing. In a recent history of the church school movement, its accomplishments were described as follows.

> The Sunday school has done some remarkable things. It led toward public, universal education. By reversing its own concept of infants as repositories of original sin, it helped in paving the way for childhood as a time of carefree innocence. Today, it continues as the major educational setting where Protestants are confronted with and urged to question the meaning of destiny and death. Approaches may often have been bluntly otherworldly or illusive, but death has been mentioned — something a public school does not, perhaps cannot, do. And the Sunday school has periodically captured and channeled aspirations of the Protestant majority by offering needed definitions of motives and goals.[1]

Today we continue in the Anglican Church to have a church school program which gathers together thousands of children each Sunday — a remarkable resource for the church's ministry with children which has developed a number of characteristics. One phenomenon over the years has been its persistency. Despite the fact that Christian educators have been pointing us toward fresh approaches to the task, building on our knowledge of how children really learn, changes in the church school program have tended to be minimal.

Another has been its lay leadership. Although many clergy are supportive of the church school, they often have little to do with actually teaching in it. Many of the problems occur concurrently with Sunday worship, so that the clergy are often excluded. Therefore, the lay tradition continues, and the volunteer teachers bring their lay theology to the task. This fact gives a great witness to the reality of Christian faith as being a factor in the everyday lives of men and women who are not in the professional ministry.

A third characteristic of the church school is the commitment and desire to tell Bible stories as a major element of the program. The Anglican tradition, with its focus on church, daily living, worship, and scripture, is a rich source of nurture and teaching for the church school. And perhaps here is a place for us to concentrate our re-awakened awareness of the liturgical importance of the Proclamation of the Word.

I believe the time has come for us to take the lectionary we use in church, with its table of lessons, epistles, and gospels, and produce teaching materials based on them. In this way children in the church school will explore the tradition at their level of ability and apprehension, as adults do the same thing in the church service. The Diocese of Colorado is pioneering in this approach, and Anglican parishes would do well to explore their curriculum program. This is especially relevant for us as we adopt a new lectionary and a new eucharistic rite during the eighties.

Dr Donald Peel, in a recent article about the two-hundredth anniversary of the Sunday School, said

> The call in this day is for new approaches to meet new forms of the old human need for reconciliation with God through Christ, and for the knowledge and power with which we can serve Him and others for Him in our generation. This demands the mobilization of all the resources, spiritual gifts, skills and experience of the entire committed membership of the Body of Christ. It will require hard thinking, inspired planning and sound theology. Do we accept the challenge? Surely we do, God being our helper.[2]

I believe that such a new approach needs to integrate children into the worshipping life of the congregation, and the biblical tradition in a variety of ways through the Liturgy of the Word. This process will make room for a teaching-learning ministry which could occur on Sundays and also throughout the week, in various settings and contexts.

The Role of Worship

Handing on the tradition finds its expression chiefly in worship itself. The fabric of Anglican liturgy is to hear the tradition in the Proclamation of The Word, and to act it out each week in the Sacrament of the Bread and Wine. In following through the Church Year, we recapitulate our tradition of birth and ministry, death and resurrection, each twelve months. The Christmas carols, the paschal candle, the liturgical colours, and the harvest decorations all add to this transmission. Preparing for and celebrating these yearly events provide stability and new meaning to the faith. When the tradition is constantly expressed and re-expressed, lovingly and faithfully in our parish churches, the second commandment is being observed.

In the new Canadian rite much greater emphasis is given to the proclaiming of our tradition in scripture. The three readings are interspersed with psalms and canticles and followed immediately by a homily or sermon. In some cases the method of proclaiming must be improved if this emphasis is to be achieved. Nervous persons with untrained voices reading unfamiliar verses must be helped to become confident, to speak with clarity, and to have some comprehension of what they read.

Various other ways of presenting the Word can also be introduced from time to time. The most successful recently at St James' Church was a seven option program where all members of the congregation chose a method to explore the same Gospel. We used play reading, discussion, art work, videotape, film, music, and sermon. Adults, youth, and children dispersed for thirty minutes to examine the Gospel passage, then we all came together again for the Offertory and Great Thanksgiving. After the service, people reported to one another over coffee.

The "Colorado Curriculum" offers opportunities for intergenerational study of the lections. These can be used in the church school before the Eucharist or as part of the service itself, as described above. Such experimental approaches, it seems to me, may help restore the transmission of the faith to a place of prominence and significance in our worship which is consistent with the spirit of the second commandment.

Excellent work is being done at the present time in the field of nurture and liturgy by John Westerhoff III. In 1970, he published *Values for Tomorrow's Children* as an invitation to dream of an alternative future for the church's educational mission and ministry. In *Will Our Children Have Faith?* (which is really what this chapter is about) he describes the parish as the vehicle and setting for transmitting to the third and fourth generation.

> Using the radical nature and character of a faith community as the context or place for Christian education means using every aspect of our church's life for education — our rituals and preparation for participation, the experience we have and provide within the community of faith, and the individual and corporate actions we inspire and equip persons to engage in. It means examining and judging our total life as a community of faith to see how well we live and transmit our Christian story or tradition, how well we minister to the total needs of whole persons in community, and how well we prepare and motivate individuals and communities to act on behalf of God's coming community in the world. This means understanding religious education in terms of a continuing struggle to reform the church.

> If we make our life in a community of faith the context of Christian education, it will mean living each day under the judgment and inspiration of the Gospel to the end that God's community comes and God's will is done. The willingness to affirm and accept this understanding is the challenge of Christian education today: it is also the basis for an answer to the question: Will our children have faith?[3]

Conclusion

The second commandment is concerned about knowing God and his/her purposes for us and for our children. We have received this "knowing" (faith) from our ancestors, and pass it on to the next generation. How we express the faith in our home and family is of utmost importance. How we use the resources of church school, liturgy, and parish to discover, explore, and express the Gospel is absolutely crucial to the life of our church in the next decade. The liturgical renewal presently going on in our church presents us with a golden opportunity to combine families and singles, intergenerational groupings, congregations and peer groups in the most exciting transmission of the tradition of belief we have yet encountered!

Notes

1 Robert W. Lynn and Elliott Wright, *The Big Little School*, (New York: Harper & Row, 1971). p. xiii.

2 Donald N. Peel, "Sunday Schools . . . Into the Third Century" *Insight*, No. 9, (Toronto, Wycliffe College, December 1980), p. 10.

3 John H. Westerhoff III, *Will Our Children Have Faith?* (New York: The Seabury Press, 1976), p. 78.

Reverence for the Name of God

Barbara Liotscos

3 Thou shall not take the name of the Lord thy God in vain

Knowing the Name

> What's in a name? That which we call a rose
> By any other name would smell as sweet.   *Shakespeare*

Living as we do in a society that relies on credit card and driver's licence numbers to establish our identity, the import of the third commandment may well elude us. However, if we approach the concept of the name in a roundabout fashion, we may recognize its continuing significance. Think of a recent occasion when you have forgotten someone's name. The ensuing discomfort swiftly turns to acute embarrassment if an introduction becomes necessary. Why have we forgotten the name? It may be that something in the situation has aroused sufficient anxiety to block our memory: our self-protecting, self conscious, "isolationist" response to a perceived threat has made us temporarily oblivious to the other. Or it may be that our unconscious anger toward the person in question has been expressed in the blotting out of their name, even as the ancients would inscribe enemy names on a pottery vessel and then smash it. To destroy the name is to destroy the person. More frequently though, we forget the name of someone whom we do not know well or whom we have not seen for a long-time, someone with whom we are lacking close contact as a person.

What's in a name? It has been said that "without a name there is no real existence."[1] More specifically, without a name, a person has no real enduring existence for us. Without a name to represent and give expression to the personal reality, we cannot remember a person. Occasionally we may encounter someone whose presence attracts us in a mysterious way, and yet their name escapes us. Then we can speak about them in general terms, but we cannot be specific. We cannot identify them for someone else, or give them credit, nor can we take the initiative to call upon that person. On the other hand, sometimes all we know of someone is their name. We have heard them talked about, but we have not met them personally. Although we may know about them cognitively, we have not known them experientially.

One day, not long ago, I was preparing to leave the church where I work, when a group of young boys came in, "to get out of the hot sun" they said, and perhaps to explore a little, too. I did not want to kick them out, neither did I trust them to stay inside unattended. So I tried to engage them in conversation, and after a while I introduced myself and asked them their names. The first boy I asked answered quickly, "Fred." "Fred," I said, "Hmm. You don't look like a Fred. Is that your real name?" Eventually the real name slipped out, and knowing his name I left them there, temporarily, much more easily. Knowing his name I suddenly had gained some power over the boy. I could identify him and hold him responsible for his actions. This is why he tried to avoid giving me his real name.

Most of us have had the experience of telephoning someone we do not know well, only to discover they are not at home and to have a stranger at the other end of the line ask our name. I have found myself at such times hesitating and responding evasively in an effort to avoid leaving my name and thereby identifying myself.

The name, then, is directly tied to a personal presence or identity. Knowing the name gives us the power of calling upon this person, addressing them, identifying them, speaking about them, and holding them responsible for their actions. Knowing the name also gives us the power of using it to our own advantage through name dropping or slandering. By such practices we may attempt to transfer the authority of someone else's name to our own.

The Biblical Reverence for the Name of God

This understanding of *name* permeates the Bible. The great amount of attention devoted by the earliest biblical traditions to etymology — that is, the derivation and explanation of a particular name — demonstrates that for them a name is far more than an arbitrary appellation. In the Bible the significance of a name goes beyond the import Shakespeare attributed to it, and the name is understood to be intrinsically related to the nature and purpose of whatever, wherever, or whomever is named. Consequently, we find that the knowing of God's name is central to the biblical understanding of God's self-revelation.

> That God should reveal his Name to His People was the most important of all gifts, the gift which contained in itself every other gift. To bestow knowledge of His Name was at the same time to grant His people power to enter into His presence to invoke Him, to commune with Him, to praise Him, and to find in the liturgical sanctification ("hallowing") of His Name, the central meaning of their own existence as His people. This was therefore something more than the revelation of knowledge "about" Himself, or even a revelation of His essence. It is a revelation of His Presence as a transcendent, personal and existential fact, indeed as the supreme actuality.[2]

Thomas Merton goes on from the above statement in his essay "The Name of God," to make the following four points. First, "the Name Yahweh expresses the simplest, most direct and most powerful manifestation of God as Person in the Old Testament."[3] Second, "Yahweh was truly a 'living God' because He was present not in a dead image, but in a powerful and dynamic personal presence, His Name, which 'dwelt in the midst of His People'."[4] Third, "to remember the Name of Yahweh was to remember all His merciful and faithful promises, all His interventions in history."[5] Fourth, "the Name of Yahweh once revealed, is a permanent promise of mercy and salvation, since in revealing His Being, and giving His Name to be invoked, Yahweh commits Himself in some sense to save a world in which His Name is present."[6] These excerpts capture the key ideas that cluster around the biblical concept of the name. The name Yahweh identifies that personal presence experienced in a people's history: the "I AM" who is present to us in our bondage will be present to us in our freedom.

In Christian thinking, the personal presence of God is so immediately identified with Jesus, the crucified and risen Lord of the Church, that we forget how this personal presence was manifested already to Israel in the name of Yahweh. This knowing God's personal presence in the Name was the context in which the apostolic writers witnessed to Jesus' divinity. It was because they had already experienced God through the Name, as the "I AM" who willed to save their people, that they recognized God's personal presence in the Christ event. The Gospel of John in particular expresses its Christology by using the divine name in Jesus' absolute "I AM" statements (John 4:26; 6:20; 8:24,28,58; 13:19; 18:5, 6,8). In the crucifixion and resurrection of Jesus, the "I AM" who is known to Israel in the judgement and deliverance of their covenant history, is made known to the nations through the apostolic witness.

Despite the centering of the Church's faith in the person of Jesus, many Christians cannot accept the idea of a personal God. For some, *personal* is equated with *human* and thus by definition cannot be applied to God. For others, *personal* also has individualistic and privatistic overtones. There is a Christian "atheism" that avoids belief in a personal God and springs from the fear of idolatry — if not through the deification of psychological needs, then through the uncritical identifying of subjective feelings, thoughts, and experience with objective reality. This weakness of the self has been described as

> the selective and unifying capacity of self-awareness especially in its historical mode as memory. The self views the present and past selectively and from what it selects it creates, relates to, and inhabits a world that is never exactly the same as the world of other selves. It does not create out of nothing, but neither does it create out of everything. And what it creates is not and cannot be an exact reproduction of the totality of what is.[7]

The spectre of human finiteness emphasizes God's transcendence and absolute otherness and unknowability, and makes any conception of God as a person who can be addressed in the direct and familiar I-You form of traditional prayer seem blasphemous. In such cases God's name has become unpronounceable, as in Israel's tradition where the fear of "taking the Name in vain" propagated the custom of not speaking the Name at all. Instead, more general terms of address were used, or reference was simply made to "the Name." To ensure that the Name would not be spoken, the vowels were omitted, leaving the unpronounceable, four consonant tetragrammaton, YHWH to stand in the written tradition. In English translations of the Bible the tetragrammaton is usually designated by LORD, as in the King James translation of the third commandment which heads this chapter. Later in Israel's tradition the vowels for the Hebrew word for Lord were combined with the four consonants of the Name giving rise to the hybrid form translated as "Jehovah," which could be spoken. This ironic outcome to the third commandment is like the case of the older child who loses a name and remains stuck for life with the baby-garbled form that a younger sibling is able to vocalize.

God's Name as Meeting Place for the Biblical Community

Hand in hand with Israel's avoidance of the Name to prevent its misuse, went the understanding that God was to be encountered in the Name. The Name was a meeting place, even as for us the eyes are the meeting place where we encounter the other and become aware of their presence or absence, their strength or vulnerability, their constancy or variability. In our own relationships, a person's name has faded in significance, and we may rarely address a person by name except in greeting, or calling from another room, or trying to catch their attention. Occasionally I have been surprised and warmed by another person's naming of me in the course of our conversation. Naming helps to alter the I-it relationship we usually fall into with people and is a reminder of the unique thou — the person — who is masked by social patterns and hidden beneath the debris of our projections and expectations. Underlying and contributing to this alienation from the other is our estrangement from our own self. Not only has God's personal presence in the Name become inaccessible to us today, but we have forgotten our own name. The recollection of the self is the goal that links such revisited spiritual disciplines as meditation and yoga with the current secular pursuit of personal awareness and integration. When we have become aware of the presence of our self, we may be able to discern the presence of that which transcends our self.

The primary significance of the Name is that it provides a focal point for the many different components in the faith community, a focal point that remains from generation to generation. The name of God is a reminder to us that in the biblical tradition, God's relationship is not primarily with an individual but with a people — a confederation of diverse groups who find their unity in their worship, through the invoking, praising, confessing, and blessing of the Name, and in their covenant obedience. "They shall be my people and I shall be their God" is the way the relationship is summed up in Deuteronomy. To speak of a personal God does not imply an individual, private approach to spirituality. On the contrary, in the biblical tradition the individual's apprehension of God is not an end in itself, but rather is put in the context and in the service of the community's keeping covenant with God through its changing historical situation. The mystics of the Bible are driven out from their solitude to confront the community and to become leaders.

In Israel's tradition emphasis is put on the corporate memory: it is the whole people who have received the revelation of Torah at Sinai. No individual alone experiences the fullness of God. Only the whole community bears the imprint of God's presence. Similarly, in the Eucharist where Christ is present to the Church in the hearing of the Word and in the breaking of bread, the body of Christ is perceived in the gathered community. One day recently I was hiking with a close friend and we were talking about the significance of her father's funeral. I had not been there, but I spoke of my own experience of funerals and how in a sense the person remembered was made present (re-membered) through the gathered presence of those with whom he had been in relationship. The images that came to mind were of the negative of a photograph, a mould or an imprint — incomplete perhaps, but discernible. One of the ways that we reverence the name of God and recover our experience of God as personal and present is in emphasizing the corporate nature of spirituality.

The Corporate Nature of Sprirituality Today

The increasing amount of time given by Christians to televised religious *programming* (in both connotations of the word) is a phenomenon that needs to be viewed critically in regard to developing a corporate spirituality. A recent survey "Spirituality in the Anglican Church of Canada," commissioned by General Synod's Long Range Planning Committee, revealed that "while only 11% of those who neither pray nor attend church regularly watch religious TV, it constitutes the third most important aspect of their practice behind private prayer and saying grace at 24 and 23 percent respectively."[8] In contrast, only 3% read the Bible and 1% receive communion. Among those who attend church and pray regularly, 57% both read the Bible and receive communion regularly, and next in popularity behind these practices is religious television, which 23% watch daily or weekly. Television's packaged religion is directed at the isolated individual, alone at home, and encourages a privatistic, one-sided spirituality that drastically reduces the real dimensions of biblical faith.

Jeremiah, in the name of Yahweh, attacked the popular prophets of his day for preaching lies in Yahweh's name.

> Is my Name at all in the minds of the prophets who preach lies, who are prophets of their own deluded thinking, whose aim it is, through their dreams which they tell to one another, to make my people forget my Name? (Jer. 23:26–7)[9]

To those rivals of Jeremiah who curried the popular support in a time of crisis and threatened destruction, and to the television preachers today, the same pressures apply.

> They are only as good as their last show. If they don't come up with the best act, the most persuasive soul savings, then they lose out to their competition.[10]

The sermon itself, adds Dr Martin Marty of Chicago Divinity School, becomes "less a religious ceremony than an extension of show business — an item in our consumer culture."[11] Harvey Cox adds to this the observation that

> The Church throughout history has acted as a moral conscience. These ministers, however, turn their back on this role. They are merely perpetuating and deepening the values of a materialistic consumer culture. They are helping people accept some very shallow values, while promising easy salvation in the most commercial setting.[12]

Two very different examples of an emphasis on the corporate nature of spirituality today are the renewal or charismatic movement, where the focus is on the individual's healing and experiencing God's indwelling Spirit in the context of the gathered eucharistic community, and the women's movement or Christian feminism, which is developing an inclusive, non-sexist language for worship to give expression to a new self-understanding and a vision of male and female wholeness. This latter goal is particularly relevant to the issue of taking the name of Yahweh in vain, for while the reform of language is a fairly straightforward task when speaking of humankind (with the exception of third person singular pronouns), great obstacles are encountered in the attempt to alter our God-language. The Lord's Prayer is a good case in point: to hallow God's name meant, on a practical level, using other terms of address, and in his prayer Jesus addressed God as "Abba" (Daddy) and not as "Yahweh" (I AM). This patriarchal orientation, which was part of Jesus' historical religious context, has contributed ironically to a situation where, contrary to Paul's vision, in Christ there is mainly male! The illusion has persisted that God is male, or at least strongly associated with the dominating male structures, since God must be referred to by male pronouns and titles, and represented by male clergy. The Church in perpetuating this illusion has misused God's name, which is truly neither male nor female.

While both the charismatic and women's movements have the power to foster community on one level, they both fall prey to the tendency to make rigid "in-group" and "out-group" distinctions and to make their own group the centre of all their thinking. This same domineering approach holds true for larger groups as well and reflects in part the need, in a world of rapid change and threatening insecurity, to seek refuge not only in the private sphere of interpersonal relationships but in the security of a group of equals. As long as we separate ourselves from other segments of the human race, through fear or greed, we take God's name in vain when we justify ourselves and our own group through "false witness" against the other. As one contemporary theologian, Jurgen Moltmann, has written with insight,

> it is not only love that is demanded. It is in the first place faith, the faith namely that the least of the brethren are waiting in Christ's stead for the deeds of the just man. It is not that the wretched are the object of Christian love or the fulfilment of a moral duty; they are the latent presence of the coming Saviour and Judge in the world. [13]

However, the survey "Spirituality in the Anglican Church of Canada," cited above, reveals that there is a common prioritizing of the Church's mission by those who neither pray nor attend church regularly, and also by those who do, that places leadership in social issues at the bottom of the list. Similarly, both groups place awareness of and involvement in community and world problems at the bottom of the list of perceived benefits of church membership.

The New Human Community and the Reverence of God's Name

In the world community, that is called for in our time in history as the only alternative to human self-destruction, no sub-group can claim our total loyalty except as part of a greater whole. The corresponding attitude is one of "cognitive respect, . . . an attitude based on the postulate of the equality of worlds of consciousness."[14] God's Name will be reverenced where "a new inclusive human community emerges";[15] where the gospel is incarnated in

> human-being-transformed
> suffering together
> gratefully graciously expectantly.[16]

God's personal presence is that constraining yet freeing power which attracts reconciliation, the "I AM" who is committed to evoking in humanity a corporate "I AM" in response.

Notes

1 G.H. Parke-Taylor, *Yahweh: The Divine Name in the Bible*, (Waterloo: Wilfred Laurier University Press, 1975). p. 1.

2 Thomas Merton, *Seasons of Celebration*, (New York: Farrar, Straus and Giroux, 1977). p. 185. © 1950, 1958, 1962, 1964, 1965 by the Abbey of Gethsemani.

3 Ibid. p. 192.

4 Ibid. p. 189.

5 Ibid. p. 188.

6 Ibid. p. 200.

7 T.R. Weber, "Guilt: Yours, Ours and Theirs," *Worldview*, Vol. 13, No. 2, 1975. p. 22.

8 "Spirituality in the Anglican Church of Canada: A Survey Analysis," Commissioned by Long Range Planning Committee General Synod, Anglican Church of Canada, June 1980, p. 19, 20.

9 John Bright, *Jeremiah*, (Anchor Bible), (New York: Doubleday and Co., 1965). p. 149.

10 Martin Marty, quoted in Timothy Bay, "Airwave Apostle," *Omni*, Vol. 2, No. 11, 1980, p. 98.

11 Ibid.

12 Harvey Cox, Ibid.

13 Jurgen Moltmann, *The Church in the Power of the Spirit*, (London: S.C.M. Press, 1977), p. 127.

14 Peter Berger, *Pyramids of Sacrifice*, (New York: 1974) p. 119.

15   Harvey Cox, *The Secular City*, (New York: Macmillan, 1965), p. 145.

16   B. Liotscos, "Position Paper on Ordained Ministry," Vancouver School of Theology, 1979 (unpublished), p. 5.

Creation and Redemption

Ebert Hobbs

4 Remember that thou keep holy the sabbath day

If God can take a day off, why can't we? It is a matter of *management*. We have all been given the same amount of time — twenty-four hours in a day, seven days in a week. It all depends on what we do with it; our use of time is a "sacramental" expression of our values and commitment. On the desk of a hotel room in which I stayed recently, there was a brochure which read, "Escape this week-end, come to the Ramada Inn," and a rate was quoted. This started me thinking about who needs to escape. Only people who are in prison, people who are not free, need to escape. Our commitments in time can be a prison, limiting our ability to be what we want and are called to be.

The "day off" is so important that it is built into the Ten Commandments.

> Remember the sabbath day, to keep it holy. Six days you shall labour, and do all your work; but the seventh day is a sabbath to the Lord your God; in it you shall not do any work, you, or your son, or your daughter, your manservant, or your maidservant, or your cattle, or the sojourner who is within your gates; for in six days the Lord made heaven and earth, the sea, and all that is in them, and rested the seventh day; therefore the Lord blessed the sabbath day and hallowed it (Exodus 20:8–11).

What is laid down in this commandment is a day of rest on which even servants are given time off from their tasks.

Strangers and foreigners visiting the household, even the beasts of the fields, are not forgotten. In its original form the fourth commandment both honours creation and is merciful to people.

It is a commandment with strong social as well as religious significance. There is an old Greek proverb which says, "The bow that is always bent will soon cease to shoot straight." During the time of the French Revolution the revolutionaries abolished everything that had to do with religion. But when they abolished Sunday, they found that they had to bring it back again. The health of the nation was damaged because there was no day of rest. Most of us know that our efficiency diminishes as we come to the end of a week and that after a day of rest we feel better both physically and psychologically. Rest provides time to restore energy, vision, and confidence, a time for prayer, reflection, and fellowship — a form of personal conservation.

There is today a new understanding of the old message that human beings are at one with all the other interrelated parts of God's creation. When God made man and woman in his own image, he gave them dominion over the earth. He made them stewards of the resources of creation, and they became responsible to God as Creator. "What is man, that thou are mindful of him; and the son of man, that thou visitest him? For thou hast made him with glory and honour. Thou madest him to have dominion over the works of thy hand" (Ps. 8:4–6). This "dominion" which is promised us in Genesis 1, and referred to in Psalm 8, does not mean that we are permitted "exploitation" for personal reasons, but rather that we, the greatest of all creatures, are committed to the care of his creation.

When we assume that we own the earth and all creation, possessiveness becomes a value we apply to the way we treat the earth and the members of our family, the way we conduct business, and the way we carry out national and foreign policy. But the biblical view is that we ultimately own nothing: we have been given the use of much, but there is a purpose and plan for its use. Our faithfulness is measured by how closely our use of our lives and creation corresponds to God's purpose and plan for us and his world.

In the New Testament as well as in the Old Testament it is

clear that the created order is God's work and, as such, it is good. God's providential care extends even to the animals, the wild flowers, and the fowl in the air. "Look at the birds of the air; they do not sow and reap and store in barns, yet your heavenly father feeds them" (Matt 6:26). In answer to the president of the synagogue, for criticising Jesus when he healed a woman on the Sabbath day, our Lord answered, "What hypocrites you are! Is there a single one of you who does not loose his ox or his donkey from the manger and take it out to water on the Sabbath?" Even St Paul, despite his rigorous Jewish upbringing, accepts the teaching of Jesus that nothing in itself is unclean. This is expressed particularly well in his letter to the Romans: "I am absolutely convinced, as a Christian, that nothing is impure in itself" (Rom. 14:14).

Creation as a Connection between God and People

The doctrine of creation is not the story of an event which took place once upon a time. It is the basic description of the relationship between God and the world. That is to say, the doctrine of creation does not presume to tell us about something that happened long ago, whose current interest for us is merely historical, but of the relationship in which God stands to the world in every moment of time. This is expressed in the fourteenth chapter of the Acts of the Apostles.

> The living God . . . made heaven and earth and sea and everything in them. In past ages he allowed all nations to go their own way; and yet he has not left you without some clue to his nature, in the kindness he shows: he sends you rain from heaven and crops in their season, and gives you food and good cheer in plenty (15–17).

The great "creation" texts of the Bible point to the basic relationship between God and the world as a relationship in which God is Lord, ruler, and owner; and we are placed in the world not as owner but as steward and manager of the resources around us. "The earth is the Lord's and the fulness thereof, the world and those who dwell therein" (Ps 24:1). How we use these resources is a mark of our faithfulness and our relationship with God.

In 1 Timothy 4:3-4 Paul commends the right use of God's gifts in creation. The New Testament suggests (Hebrews 1:3, John 1:1-4) that the whole universe is linked in a special harmony with Jesus Christ and that we are joined with God through creation.

Creation and Redemption

Creation and redemption are two expressions of the same God. In Jesus, as portrayed in the Gospels, we see certain attitudes which are basic to our approach to nature and creation. The first is a teaching that from the natural order we can gain clues of the nature of God and can learn to be children of our creator. The second is a conviction that we cannot understand these clues until we accept that creation and the continuing creative process is a gift from God. This understanding breaks through our idolatrous attachment to possessions and assumed ownership of creation, so that God's gifts can be liberated for his purpose and not exploited for our own selfish advantage.

Such a doctrine of God as Creator effects a radical revision in our attitude to our resources, creation, life, time, and the talents that God has given us. The stewardship of these resources becomes an inescapable form of Christian responsibility and Christian calling. The way we use them, and the way we manage our own lives, becomes a factor in the partnership that exists between God and us. Hence the root of Christian response to energy, the environment, the care of our bodies, must be one of stewardship. It must be one of turning away from some of the basic assumptions about economic growth and from a lifestyle based on self-indulgence. It must be the recognition of our role in God's on-going plan of creation and redemption.

Management and Justice

A most important issue for Canadians in our management of the earth's resources is that of justice. The just distribution of the wealth of Canadian resources dominates our daily news and is at the heart of the constitutional debate in our nation. As Christians, if we take seriously our calling to love our

neighbours and care for God's creation, we must see the distribution of Canadian wealth as more than a political decision.
Our attitudes toward the sharing of that wealth will indicate
our commitment to basic management and justice, principles
inherent in the fourth commandment.

We are among the wealthiest people in the world, with the
highest per capita savings of any country on earth. We are also
the highest per capita energy users. Fuel price increases in
Canada will force most people to buy smaller cars, or one car
instead of two, but in other countries they will cause starvation and malnutrition. When a higher percentage of a small
budget has to be used for fuel, less money is left for the essentials of health, food, and housing.

We are all involved in the art of living in community, but
today that community is no longer our immediate neighbourhood. It is the whole world. In the words of the Lausanne
Covenant, "We are shocked by the poverty of millions and
disturbed by the injustices which cause it." While Canadians
are among the few who enjoy unparallelled prosperity, 25% of
the world population suffers grinding poverty. This gross injustice is caused, in part, by the real connection between
resources and consumption. People often starve because they
cannot afford to buy food. They have no income and no opportunity to produce, and they are quite powerless to change their
present state.

Our membership in the Christian Church involves us in an
organization which is world-wide, capable of mobilizing and
providing both personnel and appropriate technology to enable
people to develop their own resources and at the same time to
grow in dignity and respect. As a Church we do not lack people
who are willing to commit their lives to such service. Nor do
we lack opportunities for creative and vital ministries to meet
both human and spiritual needs, although we have been reluc-
tant to share both our personal and corporate resources to this
end. Yet there is no organization in the world which can
deliver services so effectively and inexpensively! For a government to deliver such human relief it costs three dollars in
administrative and other costs for one dollar of goods delivered
to where they are needed; for charitable agencies it costs 27¢;
but for the Church it costs only 8¢ on the dollar.

The fourth commandment is not only intended to give rest to the worker but also to give life where there is death, healing where there is sickness, food where there is starvation. Initially this commandment was a form of social legislation based on religious beliefs, but for the Christian today it becomes a response to the commandment of Jesus that we love one another as he loved us.

This principle of generous and sacrificial sharing, expressed in holding ourselves and our goods available for people in need, is an indispensible characteristic of a Spirit-filled Church. So those of us who are affluent in one part of the world are called upon to do more to relieve the needs of less prosperous persons. Otherwise we would be like those rich Christians in Corinth who ate and drank too much while their poor brothers and sisters were left hungry, and we would deserve the stinging rebuke Paul gave them for despising God's Church and desecrating Christ's Body! Instead we are called to resemble the concerned Christians in Corinth, whom Paul urged out of their abundance to give to the impoverished Christians of Judea. It was a demonstration of caring concern and of Gentile-Jewish solidarity in Christ.

Lifestyle

In the economy of God, is it not possible that we, as Canadians, are called to manage our resources so that people in other places, both in Canada and overseas, will be able to live? To respond to this possibility, we are faced with the option not only of reducing the demand for energy but of changing our lifestyle. We are being challenged to adopt a lifestyle that manifests the basic values and principles of the full life in which we claim to believe and, at the same time, expresses both love for all God's people and respect for creation.

The Protestant work ethic has been a part of our culture since the days of the Puritans. It is an ethic that tilts the balance of life and achievement toward production, consumption, and the gathering of wealth. In the wider view of the development of persons and our calling to be human, a new lifestyle would summon us more to holiness, simplicity, and contentment. Perhaps an emphasis on life as a vocation is needed to replace the work ethic. Within God's plan of creation humanity has been given a particular role and a unique capacity to respond with love and respect to other people. Our Christian obedience demands a lifestyle that expresses this concern for others.

Sin, in Holy Scripture, is seen as our breaking of the harmony of the creative process. For example, the desire to use selfishly the natural resources given for the use of all people, without regard to the needs of others, is sinful. It is a condition that a National Council of Churches report calls "the perversion of dominion in domination." A lifestyle that is wasteful and extravagant in personal living, clothing, housing, travel, church buildings, is irresponsible for stewards accountable to God for the whole earth and for love of neighbour.

For a time in history we thought that the supply of creation was limitless. Now that it is dwindling away, we are becoming more aware of our poor stewardship. Our thoughtlessness and selfishness have led to the serious depletion of resources and to the earth becoming less and less habitable. We have done this as people for whom the greatest responsibility is to love. A self-indulgent lifestyle denies our trusteeship. When we pollute the air of our cities and the waters of our rivers with poisonous exhaust fumes and waste products, when we denude forests and mountains, we assume rights that are not ours. These are Christian issues — they concern the welfare of God's people and the life of his creation, they concern the survival of the human race.

It is true that the major decisions sanctioning resource exploitation for the profit of a few relate to national policy and are out of the hands of the individual, except in so far as he or she has the power of the vote. But there are some very simple things that an individual can do in response to the management criteria of the fourth commandment, as it applies to our individual lives. We can begin by not being wasteful. This applies in the very ordinary ways such as not preparing more food than we can eat, using only the water that is needed, and taking a five minute shower instead of a thirty minute one!

Better management of energy would also involve careful driving at lower speeds, turning off a television set when no one is watching, and only burning the lights that are needed in

the house. We are responsible as Christian stewards for the
health, productivity, and beauty of our natural world. We do
not have to waste, destroy, pollute, or do anything to hurt our
fellow humans. Christ marks this as "my father's world,"
created for the life and livelihood of all people, and Christians
are called to be active in seeing that it continues to be used in a
way that the Creator intended.

The Church's Mission and Ministry

The management implications of the fourth commandment
speak also to our priorities with regard to our Lord's commission to "go forth therefore and make all nations my disciples;
baptize them everywhere in the name of the Father, the Son,
and the Holy Spirit, and teach them to observe all that I have
commanded you." With the shift in population from the rural
areas to the urban areas and with the movement of people from
one part of a city to another, there has developed a new condition described in ecclesiastical jargon as "redundant
churches." These are church buildings, both in country areas
and in cities, that are not being used to capacity. With modern
transportation systems and vehicles it is no longer necessary to
have churches so spaced that everyone can walk to them, yet
thousands of dollars are being spent every year to keep these
churches open. The maintenance of redundant churches is
being carried out at the expense of mission and ministry.

There is only so much money to go around; so congregations
and other groups of people have to be selective in the way they
use their resources. As decisions are made, certain values
related to who we are and what is important to us come to the
surface. These values need to be tested against the teachings of
Jesus and his commission to his followers. In a recent study
conducted by the Joint Strategy and Action Committee Incor-
porated, using funds made available by the Lilly Foundation,
the implications of the cost of maintaining church property,
and the consequent affects on ministry and mission, were evident. Not only is there less money in the average local church,
but it is being spent in a different way than it was 15 years ago.

In 1972 an average total of 34.4¢ of every dollar spent by the
congregations surveyed was being paid to the clergyman as

salary benefits or expenses. By 1978 that same group of churches had dropped their percentage of funds used for pastoral support to 29.9¢ per dollar. At the same time the proportion for utilities rose from 7.45¢ on every dollar in 1970 to 10.41¢ in 1977. Equally as dramatic as the decline experienced by clergy in their purchasing power is the decline in the proportion these churches are setting aside for mission outreach. This averaged 21.6¢ per dollar in 1969 and dropped to 16.56¢ in 1975. In the Anglican Church of Canada giving at the parish level has just about kept up with inflation over the last ten years. However, the percentage of money that is being passed on to the dioceses, and in turn to the national structures, has fallen short of the inflation rate. This has resulted in a financial crunch that has rendered the Church unable to respond to many of the mission opportunities and expansion needs so obvious and desirable in the last ten years.

The tangible evidence of such restrictions in Canada is the withdrawal of many overseas mission workers and the necessity for clergy themselves to absorb, out of their own salaries, many of the increased travel and other inflationary costs. In short, some of the higher costs of maintaining church buildings and vehicles has been passed on to the clergy whose salaries are already falling behind the inflation rate!

A parish which did a financial review for the years 1969 to 1979 found that over those years the expenses increased 47%, the income 36%, the fuel and hydro 300%, the telephone, insurance, and postage-stationery 200%. During that time the Consumer Price Index increased 94%, the salaries were raised by 50%, and the mission outreach actually declined. This is another example of a few persons who are carrying the load of mission support in a way that should not be necessary if we were faithful to our stewardship.

Gratitude

For the early Christians the management of their resources was based on a sense of thankfulness to God for what they had received. As an act of worship they showed their gratitude by returning to the Lord the first fruits of everything he had given them. Their giving was clearly an act of worship, a celebration

of their relationship with the heavenly Father. The more we
have, the more difficult it is to be thankful. We Canadians,
among the wealthiest people in the world and citizens of a
highly technical and developed nation, tend to see ourselves as
self-made persons and, as such, do not appreciate what we
have. St Augustine once said, "Ingratitude is the devil's sponge
that wipes away all the blessings of the Almighty."

For us the management of our time, lives, and material
resources is an outward and visible sign of the values we hold.
In this way it is sacramental. The old adage that when you read
a person's chequebook stubs you know what kind of a person
he/she is, still holds true. When you look at his/her date
calendar you can also identify his/her values. Being a Christian is not a matter of keeping certain laws, it is living with a
certain attitude toward Jesus and to our fellow human beings.
Stewardship is really not a theology of giving but rather a
theology of receiving. In the words of Paul Tillich, "Religion is
first an open hand to receive a gift and second, an acting hand
to distribute gifts." If the gifts of God go unrecognized and
unappreciated, the subject of the management of our resources
leaves out the elements of both gratitude and responsibility.

Most people in North America have matured in a time of
affluence. Those things which we once thought of as luxuries,
we now consider to be necessities. We are programmed to own,
but seldom programmed to give. This is partly because, in a
highly industrial and technological society, the connection
between the Creator and the products we consume is not
clearly visible. To buy a can of corn in a supermarket does not
convey the partnership which exists between man and God in
the planting, harvesting, and processing of that corn. It is difficult to express gratitude directly and responsibly for an
anonymous gift. It is also difficult to be grateful for that which
one believes is held by right or possession. Yet, our recognition
and appreciation, as well as our response to the gifts of God, is
the basis of our Christian calling and our Christian commitment.

Overcoming what has been called the "thingification" of
life takes up a good portion of our Lord's teaching. He
expressed great concern for people who "gain the whole world
and lose their own soul." For relatively affluent Canadians the

words of Emerson that "things are in the saddle and ride mankind" are more true than we would like to think. The mystery of life in relation to our resources is that we cannot possess our possessions creatively until we acknowledge them as gifts — gifts which have a purpose for both the giver and the receiver. Seen in this light, the fourth commandment is another expression of the partnership that exists between God and his people. To take this another step further, the management and stewardship implication inherent in this commandment can be described as the main work of the church. The way we live our lives, the way we spend our time, our talents, and other resources within our control, cannot be severed from what we believe about our relationship with God.

For many years public life has been dominated by our emphasis on technology, which was often exploitative of both people and nature and did not leave much place for a theology of responsibility for creation, in keeping with the will of the Creator. Today there are signs of a changing understanding of the connection between "use" and "purpose." This developing attitudinal change could bring about a new understanding of, and faith in, God and our partnership with him, not only as trustees of his creation but as co-workers in his universal plan of reconciliation and love. The fourth commandment, with its spiritual and social implications, asserts a connection between God and people, and promises time when, through worship, and quiet reflection, we will realize again his presence and his teachings, so that we may go out with renewed strength and confidence in his presence and purpose to live another day and another week.

Note

A number of the ideas in this essay were suggested by William Barclay in his *Ten Commandments for Today* (Grand Rapids: Eerdmans, 1979).

Stuff of Other Men's Lives
Sister Constance

5 Honour thy father and thy mother

I am a great reader of inscriptions on monuments and buildings. Once when I was part of a bus group visiting the War Memorial area of Edinburgh Castle, I was almost left behind because I had stopped to copy this passage of Thucydides inscribed on one of the walls.

> For the whole earth is the sepulchre of famous men; and their story is not graven only in stone over their native earth but lives on far away, without visible symbol, woven into the stuff of other men's lives.

I've often told myself that I would gladly have missed that bus rather than lose the opportunity to add these words to my stock of sayings of "famous men." They are for me timeless, and I find myself returning to them again and again. That was back in 1972, but I keep reminding myself that I am the stuff of both my ancestors and those who are coming after me, and this puts me into a fairly frightening position — having to live really responsibly, seeing myself molded into the stuff of other people's lives.

I wonder if we do not need every so often to have this responsibility spelled out for us in so many words, possibly put before us in the form of commands. Should there be periodic calls to consider our roots, to recall wherein lies this business of remembering, and with remembering, honouring? Is this timely thinking? What says the present to these questions?

Change and the Aging Process

All around us rings out the word *change*. We hear it in every area, in every age group. Whose voice is loudest and clearest? What shall go? What shall replace? Whom shall I send? Whose are the credits? In the light of all this let us examine the fifth commandment, which reads, "Honour thy father and thy mother that thy days may be long in the land which the Lord thy God giveth thee." The first four commandments are sometimes called the theological ones, concerned with duty to God. The six that follow are called the social ones, concerned with duty to our neighbours. Is it significant that the first of this latter group, the fifth commandment, bids us to honour our first and earliest neighbours, our parents? And this with promise too! What about this giving of honour? Hear what David Hackett Fischer says in his *Growing Old in America.*

> Aging as a biological process seems to have stayed the same during the last four hundred years. But as a social process it has changed profoundly. In early America the old were fewer in number, but their authority was very great. . . . In an era when few people survived to old age, and even fewer expected to do so, the young were trained to treat the survivors with a special form of honour called "veneration" — a feeling of religious awe or reverence. Throughout the Western world, in Keith Thomas' words, "the prevailing ideal was gerontocratic; the young were to serve and the old were to rule. Justification for so obvious a truth was found in the law of nature, the Fifth Commandment and the proverbial wisdom of the ages.[1]

He goes on to remind us that honouring was not always from the heart, and he intimates that the relationship between parents and children was at a low ebb until the beginning of the twentieth century. He would seem to have supported this with historical data, mentioning the impact of two great revolutions, the French and the American, when "the idea of equality destroyed the hierarchy of age; the idea of liberty dissolved its communal base; the decline of deference diminished its authority; the growth of wealth stratification sapped its economic strength." Basically it would appear that the growing number of elderly and their longevity helped bring about a different relationship, since increased numbers brought about grave social problems to be solved only by public means. Fischer continues,

> With the discovery of old age as a social problem in the first six decades of the twentieth century, a new system of age relations slowly began to emerge. The most visible change was a radical improvement in the economic condition of the elderly, especially after the Second World War. Still many old people lived miserably, in poverty and degradation. But real progress was made after the Great Depression. Since 1940 life expectancy beyond the age of sixty has risen substantially for women. Patterns of association and residence among the elderly have changed as well, with increasing opportunities for elderly people to choose their circle of friends. And rates of remarriage of people over sixty have increased substantially. One of the most important trends in our time is the individuation of old age. A system of age relations is emerging in which age discrimination is dissolved by a respect for the individuality of young and old alike.

In all of this, where is parent-honouring? Perhaps we could say that the word *caring* best describes the new relationship between parents and children of the last half of the twentieth century. In these 1980s aging has come of age — it is everybody's concern; everybody's parents have become ours, all of us are the children, everyone will grow old. Some, like Bernice Neugarten of Northwestern University, would say that no longer is age a reliable factor in how people feel and act. "Our society is becoming accustomed to the 28-year-old mayor; the 50-year-old retiree; the 65-year-old father of a preschooler; and the 70-year-old student." Individuation or the individuality of young and old alike marks the trend of the times. It is the person, the *persona* that matters.

This brings us to see the family as the true issue in this matter of aging and honouring. It is the responsibility of the family to witness to such relationships as will edify and honour all, expressing the relationship of caring which we have come to value today.

Honouring in the Family

I was more than glad when I was searching in our library for some commentary on the Decalogue and found Carroll Simcox's *Living the Ten Commandments*, published in 1953. He chose as his title for the chapter on the fifth commandment, "On Choosing and Being Ancestors." He opened this chapter, as he seems to have opened every chapter, with a page of quotations from the pens of great authors down the ages. (This matter of honouring one's elders is no new thing!) The very first quotation, by one John Morley, was this pithy comment, "Every man of us has all the centuries in him." Following that came a great array from the pens of the great — Pericles, T.S. Eliot, Moses, Dr Charles Mayo, Isaiah, Dewey, Chesterton, the Book of Common Prayer — great names which reminded me that for a long time people in families have been bidden to mind their roots. He closed that chapter with these words:

> Honouring our father and mother begins at home, but it reaches backward and forward and spreads out. It creates and quickens that bond which embraces a longer period of time than this: a piety toward the dead, however obscure, and a solicitude for the unborn however remote. Into our homes have come from the past our civilization, our moral law, our Christianity. What will pass from us to those who come after us — the full inheritance intact and undefiled, or a few miserable tatters of what was left after we finished squandering it?[2]

What shall I say to you about this matter of honouring parents? Does it depend on who is writing? How much depends on when it is written? B.C. or A.D.? In 1953 or 1980? Since I am the one writing this chapter, listen to one in her seventies (and who must, of necessity, be personal).

I was born at the beginning of this century. I would think people were asking the same questions then that we are asking today — what shall we retain? What shall we discard? What shall we reinforce? My upbringing was flavoured by the influence of late-Victorian parents and their mid-Victorian parents. Both my parents were eldest children. It would have been their place to "set a good example" in all behaviour for their younger siblings as well as later for their own children. Honouring was very evident in both my parents — they expressed it and they expected it. But there was also affection — my mother was very fond of her father, and my father was very fond of his mother. (Both, I would say, had more formal relations with their other parent.) And this was true of our relations with our grandparents.

I had both my parents until I was fifty-one, and my mother until I was fifty-six. Honouring and loving continued. As time passed, my father became more nurturant, my mother more aggressive. We continued honouring but in a different way. Two years of illness for my father, and five years of widowhood for my mother, brought role changes, but I would say love and respect continued strong. And all of this was supported and strengthened by a large group of their siblings and friends. (I consider this highly significant.) The size of parental families and the wideness of their circle of friends was a tremendously stabilizing force. In fact we knew a lot of gracious living which unconsciously helped in the honouring process. And it imposed a challenge! To continue this "good parenting," to be channels, to remember that we are called to look both ways, to be the stuff of other men's lives, was, and still is, everyone's task. At some juncture all of us must carry the torch.

Going out from my parents and their parents, I come to "significant others" to be honoured. In my case as I grew up, this included Episcopal, Presbyterian, and Methodist ministers; YMCA and YWCA folk; Anglican Sisters working in our parish church; our teachers and professors (and the great folk to whom they introduced us — poets, artists, philosophers, educators, saints — the history makers of my race); the family doctor and lawyer; the colleagues and confidants of our families — all these helped to "parent" us. Add these all together and you have a goodly slice of humanity to whom honour is due! And all of us have some form of goodly heritage, some paths to follow, some handles on which to hold, some shoulders on which to be supported — some to whom honour is therefore to be given. And if running through it all there is a sense of the spiritual, some sense of being part of the "main," and some sense of the reasonableness of it all, does this not breed in us a call to honour? It would appear to me that somehow honouring is elicited in spite of us, and to all manner of "parents."

The Church and the Commandments

Let us now look to the Church and the commandments and see what light can be shed on this matter of accepting the admonition of any of the commandments. From time to time I worship in churches which have inscribed on appropriate panels on one side of the Holy Table the words of the Decalogue, and on the other, the words of the Creed. Somehow these buildings seem dark and forbidding. Very occasionally I attend a church service where the incumbent reads the commandments. When I ask if this is a regular part of the service, I am told that they are read every quarter or on Sundays in Lent and Advent, or before a mission, or leading up to a special sermon. One hears them as the Old Testament lesson at Matins, or as a topic for discussion for the Confirmation class. It would seem to me they have become "back bench stuff," irrelevant relevance, codes of ethics mostly ignored.

Ignored at our peril? I wonder if — in this period of new rites, avoidance of the word *sin*, of speaking only in the positive — the Decalogue and the decalogue mode are lost beneath a superstructure, shakey and watered down, the issue somehow avoided. I feel we do well to explore its relevance in the 1980s, global stuff brought to the local scene. Joy Davidman in her *Smoke on the Mountain: the Ten Commandments in Terms of Today* has this to say:

> Taken as practical counsel for survival, the fifth commandment is now almost a dead letter. Yet if our world were truly Christian, the change might be a reason for rejoicing. We no longer need our families — we are therefore free to love them with complete unselfishness. Now at last it is possible to honour our parents genuinely because they no longer have the power to kill us if we don't. The old sort of honour was sometimes an ugly sham — the son who respects Father only out of fear of punishment is not much of a son, just as the Christian who worships God only out of fear of hell is

precious little of a Christian. But the new sort of honour can be a beautiful and holy thing.[3]

Does the Church then do well to take the lead in a swing back to basics, and join forces with a society that is beginning to be oriented to this thinking? Do the '80s show a return to honouring but in a new way? I think so. Let us see.

Attention to the Elderly

Shall I say that though I neither hear nor see many dissertations on the Decalogue I am overwhelmed by the plethora of books which, to my mind, show a form of honour paid to our elderly, our parents. They are books on gerontology, the study of aging, and all the facets of this new discipline. No day without some article on the topic of aging; no week without some magazine article on the changing role of the older group; no month without some research or in-depth study of the aging process or problem. The old stereotype of the ''poor old man or woman'' is fading. Though in a good dictionary reprinted in 1954 I could find only the word *gerontocracy*, meaning government by old men, a new dictionary will give many words beginning with *geron*. That society is concerned enough to write books, and learned books too, must say something about honouring. A decade ago there were very few books in this field. Today we have a Paul Tournier on *Learning to Grow Old*, a Henri Nouwen on *Aging*, a Neugarten on *Middle Age and Aging*, a Robert Butler on *Being Old in America: Why Survive*, to name only a very few. And one can find in almost any bookstore, Cicero's *On Old Age and Friendship*. These all speak of beginning young to grow old well, of intergenerational approaches to this tremendous challenge. Can you not discern honour in this great, growing volume of literature about our ''parents'' and our ''parents-to-be''?

And one could note a similar increase in interest in aging by observing the number of conferences, seminars, workshops, and courses in the field of gerontology. Note such titles as *New Goals for a New Age*, or *Aging: We All Share the Experience*, or *It is People that Matter*, or *Rejoice in Years*. So it would seem that honouring has become society's job, and it is seen in broad approaches — in the way we house our parents, in the travelling about of the elderly, in their lifelong learning opportunities, in the health care needs. If you sit in the lobbies of nursing homes and chronic care facilities, you will see the children of the elderly come to feed, visit, or minister in various ways. The number of telephones in the rooms indicates communication. There is a growing together of the middle-aged child and the old parent.

And look about you at day-care centres, meals-on-wheels, day hospitals, longitudinal studies, gerontology classes on radio and in high schools and community colleges, imaginative housing projects, diners' clubs, New Horizon projects by the hundreds, legislation touching on improving every aspect of aging, research, pension schemes. All of this must filter down to families, to the home, to the children. Surely this is a form of honouring. "Adopt-a-Grandparent," "Grey Panthers," the "White House Conference on Aging," "The Ninth International Conference on Aging" (opened by the Prime Minister), the U.N. move to make 1982 a year of concern for the elderly — this is honouring, and a real attempt to improve the stuff of other men's lives. The move is not to put older persons on a pedestal, but to join arms with them and march with them.

And the Church? Every denomination is attempting to join forces with society in participating in this honouring. They are making surveys to find the elderly within their parish boundaries. Courses on lay pastoral visiting are part of every program for the year. Members of congregations in various professional roles are making their services known to the elderly. The Church is teaching family by being family. Baptismal services welcome newcomers into the parish family. Marriage counselling has an established place. Distress centres, day-care centres for children, kitchens of churches open to agencies. Honouring in these fields bring love, caring, knowledge, sharing. It is people who are doing these things, people of all ages.

In the research area, questionnaires show that children are concerned to live near their parents, children telephone their parents, parents have regular contact in various ways with their children. Grandchildren visit their grandparents. Most churches have visiting committees. Books on gerontology are a part of church libraries. Bible study groups in houses follow church services in homes. Churches "adopt" nearby facilities such as senior citizens' homes. If the churches are maintaining good communication with their elderly, then so are the parishioners, so are the children and grandchildren; and so honouring is done both ways.

A People Centred Outlook

And the elderly themselves. Yes, they are concerned "not to be a burden." They are helping to "run their own lives." They are returning to college; monitoring the media, the courts, the transportation systems; helping to create a truly Christian life-style. Teamwork is the order of the day. I know there are strong trends torward what has been called "community parenting" possibly because of working mothers, second and third career trends, and greater independence of seniors themselves; but there is a slow, steady return to the influence of the family. The increase in chaplaincy ministration, a move to get some form of religion back into the schools, and a strong emphasis on the Church being itself a family, and hence a family-oriented centre, says something about honouring. People are moving to a different "drum beat." It is not a command, but it is commanding people to listen, for God's commandings are our enablings. He is helping us to be creatures who can understand his will. And no generation has to begin anew. Always there have been those who honoured. Parenting is global. Citizens of every village are able to see how honouring is done anywhere in the world. Change? Yes. But understanding? Yes! "Those who put themselves in His Hands will become perfect — perfect in love, wisdom, joy, beauty and immortality," says C.S. Lewis.

Is this begging the question, book stuff, unreal? I think not. Urban living, industrialization, technology speak to smaller families, smaller homes, mobility, the "sandwich persons" — those reaching out to their young married children and on the other hand touching their aged parents. No longer are there, as says Joy Davidman again, "a hundred kinds of shared creation that bound parents and children together." There are other ways to strengthen the bonds, and they must be found in changed lives, meaningful relationships, worthy ties, honourable dealing.

My experience is limited, but in a great many "people-concerned" homes I see lots of love showered by working parents, single parents, career-oriented parents, and just plain parents. We are all being re-educated to family life. Society and the Church are seeing a new sort of honouring, "beautiful and holy." Hear again Joy Davidman.

> Once for all: if we wish our children to honour us, we must ourselves set them the example of honour . . . The ideal solution . . . is to reconstruct our own lives so that we give our children as much warmth and attention and time and teaching as the present world will allow . . . Let us drop the curious theory that the care and teaching of children are entirely women's work . . . and we might make the home a centre of Christian worship and education. But all this will not serve unless the heart is changed . . . That is the best it can ever be, without love. Let us then practice and pray for love, and the honour will take care of itself.

And we are back again to that word *individuation*. People matter, not parents or grandparents or children. Honour people, and when we see the end to agism, racism, sexism, we come to people and we will be living lives worthy to be the stuff of those who will follow us, even as we have been proud to be of the stuff of those who have gone before us. It is up to us all, whether or not we are specialists, to give serious thought to the evidence that has been accumulated in recent years, because it raises grave questions about the way our civilization is going and about the meaning of life.

It would appear that from time to time we must stop to examine our priorities and set our goals anew. I think the beginning of the 1980s is such a time, and what better gauge could we use than the commandments? The fifth deserves special consideration since many more people are living more years, families are smaller but are coming more closely together, concern is for people of every age group, and the Church is terribly aware of the shortness of time and personnel to cope with these matters. We do well then to remember that parents are more than the two who birthed us; honouring is a good and loving thing; aging has come of age, and it is a joy, a privilege, and a responsibility to be the stuff of other men's lives!

Notes

1   David Hackett Fischer, *Growing Old in America*, (New York: Oxford University Press, 1978).

2   Carroll E. Simcox, *Living the Ten Commandments*, (Wilton, Connecticutt: Morehouse-Gornham, 1953).

3   Joy Davidman, *Smoke on the Mountain*, (London: Hodder & Stoughton, 1971).

The Ethics of Death

Phyllis Creighton

6 Thou shalt not kill

Solemn, unmistakable, these four short words affirm the untouchability, the worth of human life. They mirror fear that our aliveness might be snuffed out, and awe at the wonder of our organized energy, creativity, and self-transcendence. Behind this commandment lies the conviction that our lives come from God, shaped in the divine image for relationship with God and each other. And for us now, Christ's healing of the brokenness that we create seals human worth. These four words reflect whose we are and whither we go: from love to love.

This commandment on social conduct bars us from absolute power over others; to break it is the most brazen rejection of neighbour and pretension to be God. But for the Hebrews it was a thread in a web of understandings and values linking the fabric of creation. For the biblical writers call us to govern both society and nature in ways making for fulfilled living, justice and mercy, with all people sharing in the gifts of life.

Framed in the shade of Eden's tree, symbol of our arrogance, the commandment must be lived out in the light of Calvary's tree, where Christ showed the utter love but foreshadowed in "Thou shalt not kill." As we examine these words in relation to public issues and to our own choices, we must keep before us his paradox: fullness of life comes through costly dying to self.

War

The morality of war troubles many of us. The Hebrew used in the commandment explicitly prohibits murder (taking a life for private ends), but not war. In the Old Testament "the Lord of hosts" is certainly a warrior God commanding annihilation of Israel's foes or chastising his people through their enemies. But it was the prophets' vision of God as the Lord through whom "the bow of war will be banished,"[1] of a dawn when "they shall beat their swords into plowshares,"[2] that inspired Christ, who identified his kingdom as one of love, brotherhood, and peace.

Christians have taken three stances to war: as a minority in the Roman Empire, *pacifism*, on grounds that the love to which Christ called them forbad taking life; after Constantine, *war* under legitimate rulers, for defence of peace and order; and later, the *crusade*, the holy war for the victory of God's cause. Christian acceptance of war has finally rested on an understanding that values are interdependent and that the sanctity of human life predicates liberty, order, justice, and peace. Thus kin or neighbours suffering violent attack or oppression must be defended or left victims of exploitation and destruction. In the Anglican tradition, "It is lawful for Christian men, at the commandment of the magistrate, to . . . serve in the wars."[3] The doctrine of the just war sets moral limits: it must seek recovery of possessions or rights wrongfully attacked, must promise real benefit, and must spare non-combatants. Most Christians accepted this doctrine, rejecting pacifism until recently, though Quakers, Mennonites, and other sects upheld it.

Do just war concepts fit modern warfare? In 1939 most of us were sure we had to fight Hitler to preserve freedom and humanity. Archbishop William Temple claimed then that to lay down one's life in war to defend what God values highly approximated Christian perfection in a sinful world.[4] But in the indiscriminate bombing of Hamburg, Dresden, and Berlin, and the obscene vapourizing of Hiroshima and Nagasaki, just causes turned into crusade and carnage. We have seen bestiality in the some 135 wars since then; and we cannot now evade reckoning morally with nuclear weaponry. The counterforce nuclear policies pursued by West and East rest on the willingness to unleash hideous, incalculable poisoning of the earth and mutation of the human species — apocalyptic terror. Can we conceive of having more justice, order, or dignity in the aftermath, even if such a war were fought to defend neighbours against aggression? Would it not be an act of madness and suicide, bringing appalling collapse and totalitarianism?

Think-tank scenarios, pushbuttons triggering megadeaths and unseen horrors, are demonic abstractions; bacteriological and prospective thermal weapons (particle or laser beam) and killer satellites promise further terrors. Today "the word of God is spoken in a world intoxicated by death."[5] Civil defence conferences are popular in Britain, the Pentagon asks hospitals to set aside beds for military casualties, and more and more people think the unthinkable: that nuclear war is inevitable. We now stand more in danger of war, and annihilation, than at any time since 1945 — the *Bulletin of Atomic Scientists* recently moved the Doomsday clock's hand from twelve minutes to midnight to four. With increasing political instability, flashpoints, and fear; mobile land-based and submarine-launched missiles virtually undetectable or invulnerable; Russian and American arsenals together holding massive overkill equivalent to over a million Hiroshima bombs; the risks of miscalculation, unreason, and inevitable escalation in computerized weapon systems controlled by knots of leaders; and access to nuclear weapons by more nations and terrorist groups coming, we must face our satanic potential.

In the name of God and man, we must probe more deeply "thou shalt not kill." We must pierce the myths of power. More numerous and potent weapons of mass destruction offer not more but *less* security; they will lead to heightened risk, *not* a balance of power. Nuclear war can *never* be won by a pre-emptive first strike, given the scale of retaliatory armaments. Pagan deities — Mars and Mammon — stalk our peril. The desire to "be like gods"[6] smoulders behind the temptation of leaders to make their way of life triumph by a war that they might survive. Are not the notions of resolving human problems and gaining power through war with our diabolical weapons the old temptations Jesus faced in the wilderness? Would we force God's hand to make him side with us, forgetting Christ's response: you are not to put God to the test?[7] The spiral of catch-up engaged in by the superpower blocs and their expert élites (military, industrial, scientific, bureaucratic) paralyzes the people who everywhere long for peace. It is *we* who must break out of captivity, to wrest control from nihilistic forces. Pitting the moral passion of the prophets against the clinical madness of world leaders, we must refuse to accept the present as normal. To those echoing "Man is War" we must proclaim: man, in Christ, is peace. We must ourselves incarnate that hope and reality which are folly to the worldly. "WAR IS OVER if you want it," a poster announced when Beatle John Lennon was murdered. Christians must take to heart the message IF YOU WANT IT.

The Old Testament covenant which God swore to our fore-fathers, to destroy their enemies, became with Jesus "the new testament in my blood," a radical transformation reflected in the virtues Christians preached: love, joy, peace, long-suffering, goodness, faith.[8] Many Christians, notably in the Third World, now urge unilateral disarmament, even though it might invite being overrun, particularly in Europe. Surely Christians, who know that God requires us to seek peace, justice, and freedom for all, and calls us to love of neighbour, must persist in unremitting efforts to secure enforceable disarmament treaties. We must press insistently for a halt to the production, testing, and deployment of nuclear warheads, missiles, and delivery vehicles. We must convey the realities of nuclear war, oppose hatemongering and militarism, call sabre rattling (whether Russian or American, Communist or Moral Majority). We must support peace movements and initiatives — the international observation satellite, for example; we must demand peace research and education, with substantial government funding. We are not helpless: the threat to "push the buttons" must be met with the passionate choice of life. Believing that "blessed are the peacemakers," we must foster trust, and work to forge the links and structures by which control of conflicts between nations may be attained.

Poverty

This is the more urgent since, not only is our rational grip on the world jeopardized in playing nuclear chicken, but the arms race itself exacts a heavy toll in human well-being and life. A generation ago General Eisenhower put it bluntly: every gun is a theft from a hungry, cold child. The current $500 billion spent annually for arms — one in six tax dollars — dwarfs the some $20 billion for aid to developing countries (which are also arming). Global defence spending fuels inflation, equals the income of the poorer half of the world, and absorbs the lion's share of research funds plus over a million scientists and engineers. To kill makes one culpable in senses that to let die does not, but by our choice of arms as a priority, and our failure to make serious efforts to alleviate the plight of poor nations, we are guilty of many deaths. Our brothers and sisters are dying; over half a billion are malnourished, and the number is rising; millions of abandoned children have to fend for themselves in Latin America, Asia, and Africa.

For the first time in history we have the means to meet human need, but still we choose death. The Brandt North-South report asserts that with a fraction of the resources consumed in the arms race all earth's people could have clean water, adequate food, housing, education, and health care.[9] But though the United Nation's aid target is a modest .7 per cent of gross national product, aid from the United States (where one in four tax dollars goes for defence) is only .2, and from Canada (which has a defence budget more than quadruple the aid one) .43. Worse, through trade (the major means by which money flows between nations), resources and wealth are now flowing from poor countries to the rich technological ones.

If we care about the lives of masses of our fellowmen, we must learn to think globally: their survival depends on our accepting the interdependence of nations and creating sustainable prosperity through much better trade and monetary arrangements for the developing countries, and more equitable sharing of resources. With deadlock on development issues, the rich preoccupied with recession and inflation, and Third World poverty worsening so that aid will soon have to shift to sheer survival measures, the future stands in jeopardy. Can we create the will to alter our standards of living? For the truth is, "the rich must live more simply that the poor may simply live."[10] We in affluent nations, who benefit from inequitable economic, trade and consumption patterns, should remember: if the rich insist their wealth is a right, the poor may consider their vengeance justice. Is time running out?

Revolution

Does the desperate plight of millions, and the perpetuation of poverty through political, economic and social structures — institutionalized violence, as theologians have insisted — indeed justify revolutionary violence? We worship the God of the Exodus, symbol of liberation from oppression and summons to responsible life in history. And Christ announced that his mission was to bring good news to the poor, "to set at liberty them that are bruised."[11] Comfortable Christians find it easy to preach that his kingdom is not of this world and to denounce radical action. Yet Christ plainly meant to create a new humanity, and the dynamic to make all things new *is* at work in our faith. The struggle against institutionalized violence and for social justice is profoundly ethical. Can we accept that overt violence in support of human rights and justice is moral? Many Christians in seventeenth century England and eighteenth century America did. Today we see the growing gap between rich and poor, harsh military régimes, resort to torture, and racist attacks upon liberty and life. Given the biblical call to side with the poor and overcome injustice — to realize the proclamation of God in history, not just to apply band-aids that leave evil entrenched — unknown numbers of Christians have now adopted a revolutionary stance.

But is violence an instrument of redemption, or is unmerited suffering the source of reconciling power? Though Christ identified with the poor and oppressed, he rejected a political kingdom and force; he chose to suffer the violence of the powerful even unto the cross, and by this choice gained power as the risen and triumphant Lord. So other Christians urge that only by self-sacrificial love can we create disgust for evil, show the other to himself, and compel him to live as a man — claims that ring deeply true to our faith. They insist that love alone liberates, that it rules out both violence and oppression, and is the certainty that the future belongs with justice and brotherhood. Thus, they hold, Christians must incarnate the cross, renouncing power for pardon and a mystique of hope.

But when we throw back upon God the bringing in of the kingdom, relying on Christ's transcendent power, do we in fact renounce our God-given stewardship? Do we deny the tenacity of violence in the structures of society, and the disruption entailed in its diminution? Do we run away from the reality that Christ's shalom is peace *with* justice (the two inseparable), and that, as he said, he came to bring a sword? Those who work with the disturbed tell us that gentle caring reaches someone on a rampage only if that person is first restrained from destructive behaviour. Is there a parallel here? All Christians condemn and must abstain from certain kinds of violence: torture, taking innocent people hostage, indiscriminate killing of non-combatants, the conquest of one people by another, the deliberate oppression of one class or race by another. If one remains passive in situations where these kinds of violence are occurring, is one responsible for the continuing injustice? Against the pacifist witness of Martin Luther King or Frenchman André Trocmé, there is the claim of Nicaraguan Ernesto Cardenal and other Latin American and African revolutionaries that love dictated their stand in situations of death-dealing, irremediable injustice. So we must decide whether Jesus' renunciation of violence was "a choice so basic in the definition of his ministry" as to be a continuing dictate for us, or whether in other contexts his commitment to justice and human need might lead to other imperatives.[12] I do not know if Christian faith and hope might mean choosing violent means — with the guilt and risks of dehumanization entailed — as a last resort for release from oppression. But I am sure that Christ, who goes ahead, requires us to wrestle in conscience with the ambiguities of power and with overcoming evil by love.

Capital Punishment

The other exception made to the commandment — putting to death those who committed crimes — was long regarded by Christian nations as justifiable to defend law, order, and the common good. But opposition to capital punishment as cruel, inhuman, degrading, and ineffective began some 200 years ago. In Canada, with the last execution in 1962 and with the active support of most religious bodies, it was abolished in July 1976 (except for a few offences under the National Defence Act). By 1979 seven other nations had adopted this stance, with eighteen more entirely eliminating the death penalty. But Christians are now sharply divided, some seeking its re-institution.

Some fundamentalists claim a Genesis warrant for the death penalty, to uphold the sanctity of life: "whoso sheddeth man's blood, by man shall his blood be shed, for in the image of God made he man";[13] they argue it is needed to maintain the gravity of atrocious crime. St Paul's warning that the magistrate "beareth not the sword in vain,"[14] indicates Christian acceptance that law must be backed by compulsion; but while he asserts judges carry out God's revenge by punishing wrongdoers, he upholds the sword as a symbol of authority without reference to specific constraints, and thus no warrant is provided for capital punishment. Our Lord's teaching is surely of greater significance. When they brought him the woman taken in adultery, not denying the penalty under the law he only said: "He that is without sin, let him cast the first stone."[15] And do we so easily forget how reasonable to the legitimate authorities was the unjust crucifixion he suffered so that order could be maintained over an unruly people whose own leaders identified him as a troublemaker? No, a faith forged in the shadow of capital punishment should shun it in the hope that dawned with the resurrection. Christ calls us to mercy; primitive notions of blood vengeance, of God exacting penalties, are transcended by the experience of Christ's forgiving love and promise to us of the power to redeem broken situations and people.

Given the New Testament vision of grace, can capital punishment now be justified by Christians? Opposition to it gained strength in the nineteenth century when capital offences were legion — over 200 in Britain in 1830. Modern penal systems, with alternative ways to punish crime, have been developed since then, along with knowledge about the underlying factors which must themselves be tackled: mental and personality disorders, family conflict, childhood mistreatment or injury, the poverty and powerlessness epitomized in slums. Hence experts in law, psychology, psychiatry, and social work, as well as in the churches, now oppose capital punishment. The renewed lobbying for it in Canada and the United States, in particular by the police, pleads the need for a deterrent. Yet, despite dire predictions, our quite low murder rate (2.06 per 100,000 in 1980[16]) has been declining slightly for the past four years. Our experience supports the claim the Anglican Church made more than 25 years ago: there is no ground for holding that the murder rate increases when the death penalty is abolished. It has never been shown that capital punishment has a special deterrent effect. Murders here are most often committed by a relative or business acquaintance of the victim, who are unlikely in the situation to be deterred by the death penalty; hardened criminals assume they will get away with crime. Nor must we forget that innocent people have been wrongly convicted of murder and that capital punishment is irreversible.

Murder is heart-rending; anyone holding human life precious feels horror at the deed and sympathy for the victim, their family and friends. But how can adding another broken body balance the scales of justice? Human worth is desecrated in the planned taking of life by the state, which only adds to the violence and destruction. We should never give up on a human being: as the Prayer Book teaches, God "desireth not the death of a sinner, but rather that he may turn from his wickedness, and live."[17] It is certainly a matter of grave concern that crimes of violence are increasing (as is white collar crime, which undermines the community). But the answer lies in a better correctional system leading to rehabilitation and reintegration of offenders into the community, as well as in initiatives to deal with root personal, social, and economic causes, not in a return to the death penalty.

But Amnesty International signals the gravest aspect of the death penalty for us to address: increasingly it is taking the form of unexplained disappearances, political murders, and extra-judicial executions — 500,000 in the past decade in countries such as Argentina, Ethiopia, Guatemala, El Salvador, as opposed to some 5,000 judicial executions. By mounting pressure to secure release of those detained at risk of execution, we can witness to the value of human life, in obedience to the commandment.

Abortion

Although abortion is no longer the most common method to control the numbers born, there are 30–55 million annually — one per five live births in Canada — and its prevalence rouses profound unease. Christians honestly differ on the morality of abortion. There is nothing in the Bible about abortion, but by A.D. 100 Christians, in a dissolute Roman Empire, were being taught, for love of neighbour, to shun it. Historically, the protection of the sixth commandment was extended to the child in the womb, but not always absolutely or from its earliest beginnings. Before the sixth century Christian theologians accepted a theory of delayed animation which distinguished unformed from ensouled fetus, abortion of the latter being treated with greater severity; today some Roman Catholic moralists support a renewed theory of delayed hominization of the fetus. From the fourteenth century, various theologians justified abortion of a non-animated fetus and, by the nineteenth century, of an animated one as well, to save the pregnant woman's life or even for other grave reasons. This historical development was rejected by papal decrees issued 1884 to 1895, condemning all abortion. While Vatican II termed abortion and infanticide unspeakable crimes, in Catholic theology fetal life may be taken, under the principle of double effect, where ectopic pregnancy or cancer of the uterus dictate surgery to save the pregnant woman. From the Catholic viewpoint abortion should not be termed murder; no claim to certainty about the time of animation is advanced, but rather a determination to take the surest path, extending protection to the earliest possible moment. The teaching, which is non-infallible, represents moral judgment in a complex matter allowing exceptions to the general rule, not truth revealed by God, and it ended a long tradition, unlike consistent Vatican teaching opposing contraception (which until 1917 was unvaryingly seen as interpretively homicide, on the view that it takes life before it is given). In the light of insights into the role of moral absolutes, woman's dignity and needs, and new responsibilities arising from modern medical developments, some Catholic and many Protestant theologians continue to regard abortion as morally permissible in some circumstances.

I believe we should respect the sanctity of the life of both the pregnant woman and her fetus, and also take seriously her one-flesh unity with the unborn within her, whose life can only be mediated through hers — an unparalleled situation of total dependency. The Christian tradition accepted the moral right to kill in self-defence and used proportionate reason to resolve life and death conflicts. In cases of killing in self-defence other values have been equated with physical life; bodily integrity, such supreme spiritual goods as the use of reason or saving one's reputation in vital matters, and material goods of great value have been held to justify it as a last resort, even where the assailant might not be culpable because of mental impairment. Bearing all this in mind, with the Anglican Church of Canada I accept the prime right of the fetus to live and develop but believe that right may legitimately be superseded; and I lay the burden of proof that other rights have a greater claim to recognition on those who wish to extinguish the fetus's life. The intention in this stand, which the church first took in 1967, is to uphold the value and importance of human life. Thus the need to save the pregnant woman's life, or to avert grave physical or psychological harm to her, are seen as moral grounds for abortion. For we need to reflect, Anglican moral theologian Charles Feilding suggests, on "the situation where a pregnant woman's 'life' is threatened by the risk of illness, the burden of living children, the *non*-support of society in fact, and the closeness to the 'life for life' situation in such circumstances."[18] The principle of justice underlying the right of self-defence, and the gospel call to compassion, persuade me, then, that abortion can be morally acceptable where the well-being of the pregnant woman, seen in the full circumstances of her life, can be secured in no other way.

If we hold that only the threat of imminent death justifies abortion, we deny how deeply pregnancy engages a woman's very being, and how destructive of her very life is the self-dividedness she may experience where ill health or overwhelming other responsibilities consume the energies the fetus claims. If, no matter how her body, mind, and spirit are torn, she *must* bear the fetus, then she is submitted to biological necessity and decisively denied freedom as a moral agent. We would then make of motherhood "a duty allotted to her by nature" (as Pius XI put it in *Casti Connubii* in 1930[19]) and of God a patriarchal tyrant, denying the God we know, who, giving us life and love, calls for our free response. Before we insist, on grounds that she chose the sexual union which created life, we should remember there is no infallible method to prevent conception. Further, as knowledge of genetic defects and diagnosis by amniocentesis has developed, being pregnant with a fetus with a detected serious abnormality has brought an anguish and moral dilemma unknown to previous generations. Whether one ought in sacrificial love to bear the burden of a seriously defective child, or to foreclose a destiny fraught with tragedy, is an issue confronting Christian couples not to be dismissed with either simplistic condemnation or easy acceptance. I believe Christ calls us to concern for persons in the real world, and to healing their brokenness with compassion. In that world we face radically new situations. For example, largely as a result of medical control of death, in the present population explosion many poor nations face staggering problems to provide health care and education for the unprecedented numbers of young people under 18. Reducing the birth-rate can be a case of averting malnutrition and despair. These contexts, with the claims of mercy, justice, hope, societal and personal well-being, must not be forgotten when weighing the morality of abortion. Again, technology has shifted moral dimensions for us with the "morning-after pill" which is closer to conception control; it prevents pregnancy at the outset, when the known loss of fertilized ova is high (about one-half) and before implantation establishes the secure beginnings of a developing individual embryo.

For us, as Christians, the power to create new life is a holy gift and children are a blessing to be cared for tenderly. In awe the psalmist hymns God's presence in our lives from the first days: "Thou didst knit me together in my mother's womb."[20] And with Mary, many of us have exulted in the first awareness of our motherhood: My soul doth magnify the Lord. But that same story of our Lord's birth records that, with the angel Gabriel's announcement, there was need and space for her acceptance: "Be it unto me according to thy word."[21] And that it was thought important to include this response in scripture suggests woman's assent is, finally, hers to give. Ought not we, as Christians, then, rather to concentrate on re-creating the world around her so that she may say Amen to nurturing the new life within her? With Bishop John Robinson I believe "It is on the cards that abortion, like child exposure, will come to be seen as a horror of an uncivilized age."[22] But to seek to end abortion by law is simplistic: our collective obedience to the commandment requires costlier sacrifice. To show respect for the unborn we must tackle the social dimensions of the abortion situation more vigorously. Ours is a pampered, individualistic society with too little solidarity; we give minimal welcome to children. More help for families in financial straits, suitable housing accommodation, day care, nursery schools, after-school programs, more help for children with defects, could witness to the value of the unborn. More research for better conception control could help prevent abortion, as could better educational programs and supportive services which foster self-esteem, and caring, responsible attitudes to sexual relationship and contraception.

We must never forget that the abortion procedure takes human life, that by suction, knifing, or poisoning, doctors destroy one who otherwise, in the normal course of events, would come to walk this earth, like you and me. Where a pregnant woman's real need provides the moral ground for abortion, we ought always to hope it will be sought only as a last resort, given the moral ambiguity and tragedy inherent in this act. Faithfulness to the commandment demands no less. One cannot help seeing that abortion is resorted to for trivial reasons, and also used repeatedly as a primary means of birth control by a growing minority of women. More sickening evidence of disrespect for the unborn is the claim advanced by American Episcopalian Joseph Fletcher for using live aborted fetuses for experimentation: that the fetus is a nonpersonal organism valuable only if its potentiality is wanted by its progenitors.[23] It is abundantly clear we are in desperate need of a renewed sense of that reverence for unborn life to which the first Christians gave witness.

Euthanasia

Some fear that mercy killing of the terminally ill, the senile, retarded, and seriously defective will follow legalized abortion. But further, sobered by life-prolonging technologies, many ask whether there is a right to choose death, and hope that euthanasia will become acceptable. Should we view it, then, as compassionate release or as clinical homicide?

In our day, Germany, mainly under the Nazis, carried out a horrifying program of enforced euthanasia. Also revealing and perhaps ominous are the sporadic attempts since the 1930s to legalize voluntary euthanasia in Britain and the United States, as well as the considerable public response to the British euthenasia society Exit, and the American one Hemlock, whose recent booklet described ways to bring about your own death.

Protestant and Catholic moralists, recoiling from the excesses of tubes and machinery that can rob the final days of dignity, have affirmed both the right of those terminally ill or gravely injured to refuse treatment involving undue pain, expense, risk, inconvenience, or promising little benefit, and the doctor's matching one to offer only pain relief that may shorten life; they generally regard intravenous feeding, oxygen, blood transfusion, or chemical stimulants as "extraordinary" means legitimately refused. These are important rights; otherwise treatment can torture the person and make a travesty of life. The gentler death sought thereby — the original, but no longer the current meaning of the term euthanasia — seems entirely moral. The patient is supported in facing the eventualities of an illness or injury which it is no longer reasonable to fight by medical means. This is good medical practice which respects the sanctity of life compassionately, honouring the inevitable ending written into each life at its creation; it should not be termed euthanasia at all. There is nothing morally wrong with removing life-support systems if there is no hope of restoring the patient to cerebral function. The omission of treatment for newborns with grave neurological defects (spina bifida, for instance) could perhaps be justified on a prognosis of a pain-wracked, very limited life, but is problematic because of the uncertainties of diagnosis. However, the known refusal to correct intestinal obstruction by surgery where the infant has Down's syndrome — a decision sealing the baby's death — breaks the commandment: retarded infants are persons entitled to aid needed for continued life, their potential cannot be identified, and parents and doctors deny our humanity in refusing them the care our society can afford.

What about the morality of putting the terminally ill to death? Can the fact that no cure exists, or the need for release from protracted pain anguishing body and spirit, justify mercy killing if the patient requests it? The refusal or cessation of treatment presumes an intent to let the patient die which bears some resemblance to the purpose in mercy killing. But desisting is not to be equated with doing, or permitting to die with killing. The distinction is important, not least because if we legalize mercy killing, we run the risks that the categories of the hopelessly ill or suffering would be abusively extended, the feeble subjected to pressure to seek it, and their trust in medical personnel undermined.

Doubtless under careful control mercy killing would eliminate some suffering. No moralist would condemn the bullet fired on the battlefield to release a person agonizingly trapped, and some desperate medical situations may be analogous. But what about the argument of some Christians that since life consists in mutual service, when usefulness is over and the end is near, one should have the right to choose a quick and peaceful death? Historically the Christian community regarded suicide as detestable, and while giving a lethal drug to the dying may not be abetting suicide in the moral sense, nevertheless, in our tradition, suffering and pain have been accepted as evils opening possibilities of union with Christ and of fellowship in agony. Death, our natural end, is neither to be sought nor dreaded but, rather, accepted; for life is good, and love calls us to self-giving. Christian response to disease and suffering provided the impetus for hospitals and medical care: an affirmation of life. Further, those providing palliative care to the dying tell us that the cry to be put out of one's misery is a plea for help, and when the real needs are met, the desire to have life ended very seldom persists. The commandment is based on our neighbour's claim to utter respect from us. So I believe it calls us to the cruciform pattern of life, and to rejection of euthanasia.

Personal Conduct

The intent of the sixth commandment should raise a heavy bar against war, the death penalty, mercy killing, or abortion. It should impel us to serious efforts to create a world where justice, peace and order will flourish — the biblical vision of shalom. But it reaches beyond the occasioning of actual death, for Jesus insisted it must bar us even from showing rage and contemptuous scorn to the other.[24] The heart of his claim is that violence — the root and ground of all killing — is incommensurate with our nature and God's intentions. Accepting ourselves as children of God, we are to work at reconciliation and peace: this is the thrust of the prohibition against taking life.

The other side of the coin, for this commandment, is God's affirmation that our creation is good, and the promise of life in all its fullness given through Christ. So we are bidden by it to reflect on whether we give life to others or behave destructively toward them. We need to think about how we can crush those near us by our harsh criticism, or by laying down heavy rules or judgments and thus undercutting their search for themselves and responsibility. Seeking revenge for grievances; dishonesty; passive refusal to give hope, trust, and encouragement to someone who needs it; self-absorption so that we are deaf and blind to all but our own troubles — all these can undermine those near us. We must learn to listen, support and comfort others, especially those in trouble; to hear their pain, bewilderment, rage or grief; and to help them live with independent integrity. In all this we need to take seriously that "there may be many accidental deaths caused by our failure to realize the power of life and death we actually have over others."[25]

We know that violence as a solution for human dilemmas

is incommensurate with our nature: the tree of Calvary is the final answer to the tree of Eden. As Christians, we stake our lives on the belief that we are made for self-giving in love that does not count the cost. For we know we are called to find life through losing it, graced, by the God of love who gives us hope in Christ, to live out the profound paradox of the cruciform shape of reality. Thus we will take our place in the renewal through which God is overcoming death with life.

Notes

1 Zechariah 9:10, Jerusalem Bible.

2 Isaiah 2:4, also Joel 3:10, Micah 4:3, King James.

3 Article XXXVII.

4 *Thoughts in war-time* (London: Macmillan & Co. Ltd., 1940), pp.33–34.

5 Daniel Berrigan, cited in "Passover and Easter: a sharing of liberation by Jew, Christian," *Globe and Mail* (Toronto), 17 April 1981, p. 7.

6 Genesis 3:5. Jerusalem Bible.

7 Matthew 4:7 Jerusalem Bible.

8 *see* R.H. Bainton, *Christian attitudes toward war and peace: a historical survey and critical evaluation* (Nashville, Tenn.: Abingdon Press, 1960), pp.55–56.

9 *North-South: a programme for survival*, ed. Willy Brandt (Cambridge, Mass.: M.I.T. Press, 1980), pp. 14, 118; *see* also Ernie Regehr, *Militarism and the world order: a study guide for churches* (Geneva: the World Council of Churches, 1980) p. 46.

10 Charles Birch in an address to the World Council of Churches' Fifth Assembly, 1975, cited in Ronald Sider, *Rich Christians in an age of hunger: a biblical study* (Downers' Grove, Ill.: Intervarsity Press, 1978), p. 171.

11 Luke 4:18, King James.

12 *Violence, nonviolence and the struggle for social justice* (Geneva: the World Council of Churches, 1973), p. 12.

13 Genesis 9:6, King James.

14 Romans 13:4, King James.

15 John 8:11, King James.

16 Statistics Canada [85-209], "Preliminary 1980 Homicide Statistics," (mimeo).

17 The absolution, Morning and Evening Prayer.

18 personal communication, 7 June 1975.

19 cited in J.F. Dedek, *Contemporary medical ethics* (New York: Sheed and Ward, 1975), p. 118.

20 Psalm 139:13, New English Bible.

21 Luke 1:38, King James.

22 "Abortion," in *Christian freedom in a permissive society* (London: SCM Press, 1970), p. 66.

23 cited in J.T. Noonan, Jr, *A private choice: abortion in America in the seventies* (New York: the Free Press, 1979), p. 119.

24 Matthew 5:21–26.

25 Eugene Kennedy, *A sense of life, a sense of sin* (Garden City, N.Y.: Doubleday & Company, Inc., 1975), p. 137.

Toward a Healthy Sexuality

James Reed

7 Thou shalt not commit adultery

That sexuality is alive in contemporary society needs no debate! Our media in its many forms constantly bombards us with stories about people who are expressing themselves sexually in a variety of ways and at many different stages in their lives. Public debate proclaims the virtues and vices of "open marriage," "comarital sex," "swinging," "group marriage," "communal living" — to name but a few options. Personal conversations, not infrequently, are filled with serious comments and light-hearted jokes about our sexuality.

Whether sexuality is alive *and* well, however, is a highly debatable issue. The same media also reports some of the distortions that result from various kinds of sexual activity. Some of these distortions are rooted in drives and choices involving violence, oppression, and illness. While public debate tends to give an unbalanced view of the virtues and vices of some sexual lifestyles, it often underplays the significant turmoil in people's lives caused by a "laissez-faire" approach to sexuality. Personal conversations also turn to the hurt, alienation, mistrust, disruptions, and guilt flowing from some kinds of sexual expression.

The intention of this brief article is to examine some of the major understandings of sexuality within the Judaeo-Christian tradition. It will do this in the light of the seventh commandment — "Thou shalt not commit adultery." While this commandment, like many others, often is viewed in terms of what it prohibits, it also can be approached from a standpoint of what it implys as an ideal about living sexually in a responsible and healthy manner. In this case, the commandment strives to say many positive things about the nature of sexuality, its relationship to marriage, and our quest for human wholeness as sexual persons. The commandment is more than prohibition. It points us toward a healthy sexuality.

This article will be divided into six sections. The initial four of these will outline traditional teaching about sexuality and its relationship to marriage and adultery. Then there will be a discussion about some possible limitations of such viewpoints. A concluding section will discuss moral decision making. This article then will attempt to provide the information necessary to think seriously about our sexuality and to make responsible decisions about it. In no sense, however, will it be a "how-to" manual.

Some Meanings of Sexuality

A central part of who we are as humans is our sexuality. Although sexuality is greater than any definition of it, it might be considered under two broad headings. These might be referred to as *essence* and *behaviour*. The essence of our sexuality includes our erotic attraction to and preference for members of the same or opposite gender. Sexual behaviour, on the other hand, refers to the ways we act upon our sexual essence. It takes account of how we behave as sexual persons. Put another way, the essence of our sexuality is a natural part of the created order of life; sexual behaviour is the result of our choices as persons who are decision makers.

Elaborating such distinctions in a search for ways to express what we mean by our sexuality, a recent study on human sexuality has these things to say about it.

Sexuality, while not the whole of our personhood, is very basic and permeates and affects our feelings, thoughts and actions. Sexuality is our self understanding and our way of being in the world as male and female. It includes attitudes about our bodies and those of others. Because we are body-selves, sexuality constantly reminds us of our uniqueness and particularity: we look different and feel differently from any other person. Sexuality also is a sign and a symbol of our call to communication and communion with others. The mystery of our sexuality is the mystery of our need to reach out and embrace others, physically and spiritually. Sexuality expresses God's intention that we find our authentic humanness in relatedness to others.[1]

Seen in such a light then, sexuality is much more than what we do with our genitals. It is more than behaviour. As people who live within our bodies, we experience the emotional, cognitive, and physical needs for "communion" with others. As such, every human being is a sexual person — young and old, single or celibate, divorced or widowed, disabled or virile, and so on. The essence of who we are is sexual. How we act or behave about this needs to be informed by principles which are life giving rather than life denying. How then do we celebrate ourselves as sexual persons?

Theological Understandings of Sexuality

When we consider both the essence and behaviour of sexuality from a theological perspective, we quickly see that it is understood in at least four basic ways. These perspectives are found within the Bible as well as the traditional doctrinal and moral teachings of the Church throughout history. They also are considered from a standpoint of "contemporary reason."

The first of these perspectives deals with the unity of persons. In creating humans, God creates us as whole beings. We are not divided into different components nor are we spirits to whom bodies are temporarily or accidently attached. Our sexuality therefore is a part of all of who we are and is not only one part for us — be that physical, erotic, psychological, social, or religious. We are one, and our sexuality is central to who we are as persons.

A second theological perspective on sexuality is its intrinsic goodness. There is no way in which it is fundamentally evil, even though the ways we express our sexuality might cause great distress. In creating us as sexual persons who are whole persons, God values sexuality as good, blessed, and purposeful.

So God created man in his own image, in the image of God

created he him; male and female created he them. And God blessed them and said unto them, be fruitful and multiply, and replenish the earth . . . . and God saw everything that he had made, and, behold it was very good (Genesis 1:27–31).

A third theological perspective on sexuality illuminates our understandings of the consequences of sexual behaviour. The effects of the ways we choose to act sexually are both individual and collective. While sexual acts release various tensions, stimulate various sensations and fantasies, as well as involve biological functions, they involve much more than that. They are a deeply personal way of communicating with another person, or being "in communion" with another person. Sexual acts can unite us in a highly distinctive manner. In this sense, they are a special way of knowing another person and being known by someone else. We see this in the Bible when the word *know* is synonymous with intercourse.

Now Adam knew his wife; and she conceived, and bare Cain, and said I have gotten a man from the Lord (Genesis 4:1).

The consequences of "being known" in this case are obvious. Sexual expression is both an act of communion and procreation. While the latter, of course, is not always the result of sexual intercourse, the act of "communion" within that intercourse is a deeply personal way of relating with another person. As such, it also has social implications. Knowing this, the early Jewish and Christian communities set clear standards for appropriate behaviour. These communities knew that sexual acts did not simply concern the individuals involved. They also had many implications for the wider community.

A fourth theological perspective in sexuality reminds us that we experience much ambiguity in our lives. While knowing communion, we experience alienation; while feeling free, we experience boundaries; while being fulfilled, we experience limits. As sexual persons, we experience both health and brokenness. As an inescapable part of our persons, sexuality inevitably is involved in such ambiguities. The Bible and Church history record innumerable examples of rape, sexual exploitation and oppression, impersonal sex and infidelity. They, of course, also tell stories involving the joy and fulfillment of persons who experience and express their sexuality.

In view of such theological perspectives, we might consider some purposes of sexuality. There are at least four.

First, to be human is to long for community — with others and the divine. Our sexuality expresses both the need and desire for this community or communion. It contributes to the unitive forces of life and enhances our communication with another.

Secondly, as an expression of communion, our sexuality also can be an act of procreation. While enabling us to experience special union with another, our sexuality can be an opportunity to create new human life on behalf of the divine.

Thirdly, as expressions of communion and of procreation, our sexuality is an opportunity to experience fulfillment and human wholeness. While it has the potential to distort our personalities in profound ways, our sexuality is intended for our well-being.

Fourthly, our sexuality is a call to exercise Christian love. In searching for communion, in acting procreatively, and in experiencing human fulfillment, we ponder how our sexuality nurtures and sustains Christian love or how it diminishes or eliminates it.

Sexuality and Marriage

As people strive to live out the purposes and meanings of their sexuality, they soon realize the importance of the context in which these are experienced. Does that context lead to a deepening sense of fulfillment, respect, and mutuality, or does it result in increasing emptiness, exploitation, and powerlessness? There is, of course, no easy answer to such a question.

While there are different contexts in which sexuality can be expressed, the Judeao-Christian tradition has argued that marriage is the most consistently reliable one. Stated succinctly by the General Synod of the Anglican Church of Canada in 1980, "Christian marriage is a way of the Spirit through which the wholeness of human sexuality is offered to God."[2] Before considering any challenges to this, let us at least briefly look at some Christian meanings of marriage and how these provide a healthy context in which to express the joy and fullness of human sexuality.

There are many theologies of marriage and sexuality. One representative viewpoint might be stated as follows.

Christian faith affirms marriage as a covenant of fidelity — a dynamic, life-long commitment of one man and one woman in a personal and sexual union . . . . Marriage is not simply a legal transaction which can be broken when the conditions under which it was entered no longer exist. It is an unconditional relationship, a total commitment based on faithful trust. This union embodies God's loving purpose to create and enrich life . . . . Marriage is ordained by God as a structure of the created order. Thus the sanction of civil law and public recognition are important and beneficial in marriage, as checks against social injustice and personal sin . . . The relationship between husband and wife is likened in Ephesians 5:21–23 to the relationship between Christ and the church.[3] This depicts a communion of total persons, each of them living for the other. As with the covenant between Christ and the church, the promise of fidelity is fundamental. Therefore, Christians regard marriage as a primary setting in which to live out their calling from the Lord.[4]

Such a statement deserves much reflection. In outlining a great deal about the inter-relationships between marriage and sexuality, it raises at least three images about human relationship. These are *covenant*, *journey*, and *sacrament*.

Covenant refers to a particular dynamic relationship between God and a chosen community of people throughout history. It also is a model for human interaction. It calls relationships to be built on trust, truth, and clear expectation. "Trust is necessary to hold relationship together, truth is necessary to maintain productive communication and mutuality of interest, and clear expectation is necessary to keep the relationship on a common course and prevent it from serious disruption and misunderstanding."[5] These qualities are basic to both a healthy marriage and sexuality.

Journey is an unfolding or becoming. It is shaped by its beginning points, its destinations, and many things known and unknown along the route. It will include joy and pain in varying degrees and probably some significant surprise. Marriage and sexuality are not unlike this. The history of the persons, individually and as a couple, are important. The things they want to experience and accomplish suggest many directions for the expression of their marriage and sexuality. The ways they approach the known and unknown will either cultivate or withhold many kinds of fulfillment. The capacity for surprise and spontaneity will enable them to experience marriage and sexuality as a gift.

Sacrament is more abstract and less concrete. It refers, though, to the inter-relationships of the inner and outer parts of life — of sign and action. As persons with bodies, we have a capacity to love that is not separated from our sexuality. Our ways of loving say much about our sexuality. In marriage we have a way in which an embodied love is both known and expressed most fully. One author has put it this way:

> The uniting of man and woman in marriage has made possible an approved way to develop those qualities of love upon which we have insisted, the giving and receiving relationship, the mutuality, etc., are all given a setting which makes it much easier to grow in them towards fulfillment. Sexuality so conceived has been raised by Christian instinct to the level of a sacrament of the church . . . . by some deep insight the Christian church saw how such a sexual relationship could be, and was, a token of God's presence as Love.''[6]

Marriage as a context for special expressions of communion and procreation call sexuality to become sacrament.

Adultery and Fidelity

When we view adultery within all these understandings of sexuality and marriage, we easily can see how straightforward the meaning of it is. It is sexual intercourse between a married person and someone other than that person's spouse. Put another way, a married person who has sexual intercourse outside of marriage is committing adultery.

Traditional moral teaching says that an adulterous relationship cannot fulfill all the purposes and meanings of sexuality and marriage in a responsible manner. All patterns of sexual behaviour outside a relationship bonded in marriage are considered wrong, regardless of circumstances. This is so because the essential purposes and meanings of sexuality and marriage are not being met.[7]

The strength of such an approach lies in its fidelity to a carefully and sensitively developed understanding of sexuality and marriage. One author says this:

> Whether adultery is accidental or intentional, clandestine, ambiguous or consensual, the overwhelming evidence is that it is harmful to truly meaningful, loving, committed, monogomous marriage. 'Thou shalt not commit adultery' is not only moral but necessary if monogamous marriage is to survive.[8]

Within such a position, serious consideration might also be given to "creative growth" for individuals, the "human integrity" of each individual, as well as the possible positive effects of adultery upon an existing marriage — in certain cases. The conclusions of such considerations, however, would be that extra-marital sex is wrong. It splits energy for loving between two relationships and ultimately means that justice is done to neither partnership.

The Tradition in the Future

While there is a very great deal of wisdom in the traditional understandings of sexuality and marriage, there are some serious questions which might still be considered. Raising such questions, of course, does not mean the automatic elimination or downgrading of traditional teaching and morality. Rather, challenges to a tradition hopefully clarify its appropriateness and encourage both those who adhere to it and those who do not, to appreciate its basic worth.

When there is an uncritical equation of sexuality and marriage, there can be some very harmful consequences. People can wound each other very deeply when blind adherence to a code discards sensitivity and compassion.

> In recent years, Christians as well as humanists have begun to indict 'traditional monogamy' on a variety of counts: its wedding to the nuclear family form; its failure to meet the growth needs of partners through its inherent possesiveness;

its propensity toward continuing sexual inequality; its cultivation of a vivid sense of failure when one partner cannot meet all the other's needs or when the relationship itself must be terminated.[9]

Such a statement, of course, does not invalidate traditional teachings on sexuality and marriage. It does, however, call us to look seriously at the abuses which can result from such a viewpoint when it is lived out in an insensitive manner. Loving in sexuality and marriage evokes power, power which can be expressed constructively or destructively.

While there is much evidence that adultery is hurtful to all the people involved in it, there are some instances when it has deepened personal understandings and commitments as well as having awakened significant new spiritual dimensions. There are people who, in sharing their lives with someone other than their spouse, discover that a special expression of their mutual care and "communion" is experienced in sexual intercourse. They do this, knowing that they are breaking a tradition which teaches that intercourse outside of marriage is wrong. They are not caught up with naive narcissistic creeds that proclaim the goodness of "recreational sex," "doing your own thing," or "anything goes as long as no one gets hurt." They are suggesting that, under certain limited circumstances, sexual intercourse which upholds the unitive purposes of sexuality (i.e. communion) within the tradition can be both enriching and responsible. This is made possible, in part, through contemporary contraception which removes the procreative aspects of sexuality, the fears of pregnancy, and the accompanying concerns about child rearing. Such people do not boast about the "rightness" of their behaviour. While recognizing a breach with tradition, they also wonder about the "goodness" of their relationship and ponder how "grace" is experienced within it. Simply to tell such people that they are "wrong" does not enlighten traditional understandings of sexuality and marriage, nor does it encourage responsible ethical choice which issues in love and justice.

When sexual behaviour is linked exclusively to marriage, there is a large segment of society which is forced into positions of ethical choice which sometimes are fundamentally intolerable for them and sometimes can leave them with destructive guilt and/or repression as well as lowered self esteem. These are people who, sensitive and responsive to traditional teaching about sexuality and marriage, automatically have no choice but abstinence. Their decisions, in some very real respects, are made for them by the tradition, and they are denied the right to make a conscientious moral choice. Such people are the widowed, the deserted, the disabled (inside and outside of institutions), and those who have chosen, for various reasons, to be permanently single. There also are those who have become aware that they are homosexual. While they might not always know why they are so, they realize that this is who they are, after considerable self examination, and accept that as "good." Jessie Bernard, in her thorough and balanced study, *The Future of Marriage*, states that marriage has a clear future in our society. This is so, she argues, because men and women will continue to want and need the lasting bonds of intimacy and mutual support. In other cases, they also will want children and the accompanying, supportive, stable environment for their nurture. "Still," she adds, "I do not see the traditional form of marriage retaining its monopolistic sway. I see, rather, a future of marital options."[10] While traditional marriage will remain one of these options for many people, there will be others. Such options will permit different types of relationships at different stages of life as well as a variety of living arrangements depending upon the nature of those relationships.

One of the challenges inherent in all of this is how traditional Christian principles about sexuality can inform and enlighten alternate lifestyles without resorting simply to a dogmatic plea for abstinence. How can we be responsible about our sexuality outside of marriage, given a "single state"?

Making Moral Decisions

While the foregoing comments raise questions about some parts of traditional teaching on sexuality and marriage, they do not overthrow it. Rather, they challenge us to recapture what the essential principles within it are and how these enable us to make responsible moral decisions.

By way of summary, the tradition teaches that sexuality is intrinsic to every person and that it is good in itself. It expresses our desires for "communion" with another and for procreation. It calls us to perceive a mystery within sexuality which is divine gift. It points toward a continuing experience of grace in our relationships. It also summons us to express love and justice in all our sexual behaviour. What then are love and justice within sexuality and how do we determine them?

C.S. Lewis in a book entitled *Four Loves* points out four kinds of loving. First, there is *charity* which is a fundamental respect. Next, there is *eros* which is the sensual attraction and desire for fulfillment. Thirdly, there is *philia* which is general friendship and mutuality. Finally, there is *agapé* which is self-giving or other-regarding love.

> Authentic sexual love is multi-dimensional and involves all of these. It is respect and caring. It is attraction to another and the desire for sexual and personal fulfillment in and through the other. It is friendship and mutuality based upon an affectionate community of concern and shared interests. It is desire to give to another out of the fullness of one's own personality and the willingness to receive from the depths of the other to whom one is committed in a close, trusting and faithful relationship. [11]

As we attempt to exercise these kinds of loving, we also need to be aware of the power within sexual expression and how this can lead to different kinds of exploitation. Eric Fromm in his classic book *The Art of Loving*, reminds us of the inter-relationships between loving and justice. Loving that leads to exploitation is devoid of justice and ends in sentimentality. There are numerous examples of this within the current debates on what it means to be masculine and feminine. Justice which dismisses loving falls short of justice itself. A classic example of this is found in cultures where a wife is regarded as her husband's property and her adultery is a violation of property rights. Love and justice together do not tolerate double standards.

Love and justice within sexuality require a careful examination of the real nature of a relationship and the covenants within it. James Nelson outlines one way of evaluating such covenants.

> They will be covenants — and not simply contracts. They will be enduring covenants — pledges of ongoing faithfulness to the well-being and growth of each partner. They will be covenants of intimacy — in which eros is undergirded, infused, and transformed by agapé. They will be sacramental covenants — whether or not officially sacraments of the church, they will yet be those unique arenas in which the humanizing love of God is vividly experienced. And they will be covenants which, in one way or another, genuinely enlarge the partner's capacity for communion with others and expand their willingness to be part of God's work of giving new life and renewal to the world.12

Love and justice within our relationships also call us to self examination about how we make moral decisions. There are at least four basic elements within such a process.

The first of these involves our *motivation* in any action. While each sexual act should be motivated by love and justice, there are times when it is not. We need to ask ourselves what is really prompting us to act in a particular way. Is it actually an expression of love and justice?

The second of these concerns *objectives*. While every sexual act should strive to contribute to the wholeness of the people concerned, there are times when it does not. We need to ask ourselves whether this act will really contribute to a sense of being at one with oneself, with the other and with God.

The third element in a moral decision is an assessment of the inherent rightness or wrongness of particular kinds of *behaviour*. While sexual acts should never be debasing, exploitative, harmful, or cruel, there are times when they are. We need to ask ourselves searching questions about what it means to be a healthy person in any particular act.

The fourth area of concern within a moral decision includes concern for the *outcomes* of behaviour. What will happen when I do this? Marks of love and justice within sexual behaviour are the levels of responsibility which each person takes for the other in terms of emotional well being, religious nurture, and cognitive development.

A healthy sexuality then is one which experiences the joy of living with value and meaning; it is informed by a theological perspective which enlightens our understandings of the purposes of sexuality; and it strives to express love and justice in relationship with another.

Notes

1 *Human Sexuality: A Preliminary Study* (New York: The United Church of Christ, 1977), p.87.

2 *Committee on Marriage and Related Affairs*, General Synod, The Anglican Church of Canada.

3 Ephesians 5:21-23: "Be subject to one another out of reverence for Christ. Wives, be subject to your husbands, as to the Lord. For the husband is the head of the wife as Christ is the head of the church, his body, and is its Saviour."

4 "Social Statements of The Lutheran Church In America"; The Fifth Biennial Conference, Minneapolis, 25 June-2 July 1970.

5 James Wilkes, *The Gift of Courage* (Toronto: Anglican Book Centre, 1979), p. 33.

6 Norman Pittenger, *Making Sexuality Human* (New York: Pilgrim Press, 1979), p. 51.

7 Warrants against adultery: Exodus 20:14; Deuteronomy 22:22; Mark 10:19; John 8:1-11.

8 F. Philip Rice, *Sexual Problems In Marriage: Help From A Christian Counsellor* (Philadelphia: Westminster Press, 1978), p. 148.

9 Anthony Kesnick, ed., *Human Sexuality: New Directions In American Catholic Thought* (New York: Paulist Press, 1977), p. 150.

10 Jessie Bernard, *The Future of Marriage* (New York: Bantam, 1973), p. 301.

11 *Human Sexuality: A Preliminary Study*, p. 103.

12 James Nelson, *Embodiment: An Approach to Sexuality and Christian Theology* (Minneapolis: Augsburg, 1978), p. 151.

Private Property, Inequality, Theft

Anthony Waterman

8 Thou shalt not steal

We can only "steal" something that belongs to someone else. The commandment against stealing therefore implies a right to own property. If individuals and families may exercise this right, then inequality must result. For human life is a struggle for survival and power, and we differ widely in our ability to compete. Those who fail the standards of our time and place are doomed to poverty. These considerations caused Proudhon to utter his famous paradox: property is theft.[1]

There are two ways to resolve the paradox. Either we could vest all property rights in the state, as in totalitarian socialism; or we could abolish property altogether, which was the romantic, anarchist solution favoured by Proudhon himself. For reasons I shall make clear in this chapter, it is my opinion that neither of these solutions is available to the Christian in the eighties. We are stuck with the paradox. There is no justification for the inequality which produces poverty, and there is no merely political solution to the problem.

I begin by developing the argument that private property leads inevitably to inequality and poverty. Next, I try to show that the Christian Church has always upheld some more or less qualified right to private property and has generally been willing to settle for the resulting inequality. Lastly, I appraise some putative remedies for poverty.

Private Property and Inequality

Aside from gifts and transfer payments, our incomes are the sum of what others give us for the goods and services we produce for them. It follows that the size of one's income is given by two factors: the quantity produced and the value others place on that output.

A worker's ability to produce is itself a compound of many things. Some of these are personal and individual, such as health, strength, education, and ambition. Others are external to the individual, such as climate and weather, quality of soil, and the machinery and equipment he has to work with. More subtle influences too, such as religion, law, custom and tradition, social attitudes and expectations, have a part to play. An Englishman who migrates to Canada may double his productivity — and therefore his real income — without any change in health or training. Some of his larger output comes from using newer and more powerful equipment, and some from more effective management and work supervision. But much is due simply to the social environment of North America, where work is regarded with approval and where, therefore, a man can put in eight honest hours a day without disloyalty to his mates.

Production takes place when men and women work with land, materials, and equipment. As well as "hands" we need factories, warehouses, stocks of goods, farm land, roads, vehicles, and telephones. All these other, non-human "factors of production" have to be paid for. Someone has to produce them or make them available by taking them out of alternative use. Part of our income, therefore, is the result of the work we do ourselves, and the remainder is payment for the use of those productive facilities we happen to own. Suppose a farmer makes an annual revenue of $50,000 net of production costs and expenses. If another owns the land, he must pay (let us say) $10,000 rent. His income from *work* is thus $40,000. If he owns the land himself, his total income is $50,000, $10,000 of which is income from *property*. As productive wealth accumulates over the generations a larger absolute amount (though not necessarily a larger share) of total income from production is paid to the owners of property. In Canada in 1978, a total of about $57 billion, some 20% of gross national product, was paid to property owners in the form of rents, interest, and profits.

Ability to produce, either by one's own hard work and skill or with the productive resources one owns, is only half the story however. The other half is the valuation placed by society on what one produces. Suppose a pop-singer or hockey star earns $1 million a year compared with a doctor's income of $100,000 and a clergyman's of $10,000. Society values the entertainer's weekly man-hours at about ten times those of the doctor, and the doctor's at about ten times those of the clergyman's. These valuations are partly governed by relative scarcity, partly by taste and technology. If every adult male could play hockey as well as Bobby Hull, the NHL could buy its players' services at the minimum wage. As teenage devotion to crooners is replaced by even greater devotion to rock musicians, the incomes of the former fall relative to those of the latter. The invention of computers degrades the economic and social position of book-keepers and exalts that of technicians.

Now it is evident that we come into this life very differently endowed with the personal qualities which affect productivity. We differ moreover in the wealth we inherit, the quality of our education and upbringing, and the social environment in which we form our attitudes and expectations. Furthermore, we are exposed to unpredictable fluctuations in the demand for our goods and services. It is not to be wondered, therefore, that the national cake is very unequally sliced. The richest 20% of Canadian families got 42.5% of national income in 1978; the poorest 20% got only 3.9%. Estimates of the number of Canadians living in poverty in 1978 range from 2.8 million (Statistics Canada) to 4.4 million (Canadian Council on Social Development).

If everyone inherited the same (small) capital, had the same education, grew up in the same kind of family, and enjoyed perfect health and immunity from accident, there would still be differences in income. The more industrious and talented (and aggressive) would rise to the top: the idle and incompetent (and kindly) would sink to the bottom. Chance variations in demand would produce fortunes for the lucky and redundancy or bankruptcy for the unlucky. But the income range would not be so wide, for productive abilities are nurtured, not innate. Moreover, with a reasonably competitive economy the effect upon incomes of changes in society's valuations would be largely offset in the long run by appropriate shifts in the pattern of production and employment (though some "windfall" redistributions of wealth would remain). Inequality could thus be explained as a necessary cost of economic efficiency. Inasmuch as society valued efficiency (or "stewardship") in the use of this world's goods, the corresponding distinction of rich and poor could be perceived as "just."

What makes inequality a permanent and hereditary feature of our society, divorcing it from efficiency and taking away its moral justification, is private property. This is not only or even chiefly a matter of money. If total property income in Canada were equally shared, the annual proceeds per family in 1978 would have been about $3,500. Though the large property incomes of the very rich would have been drastically reduced, and the incomes of the 16% of all families earning less than $5,000 roughly doubled, the great majority of Canadian families would have been relatively unaffected. The significance of the accumulation and hereditary transmission of private property lies more in its cultural and social effect.

In the first place, of course, the income we get from our property is often far greater than its dollar value. Books, pictures, a spacious house and a summer cottage yield no cash return. But they afford us a flow of satisfaction which is quite as much "income" as a monthly pay-cheque. The market value of that "income" is implicit in the price at which such assets change hands, but it forms no part of "national income" as estimated by Statistics Canada. Property income is therefore grossly underestimated in the National Accounts. Since ownership of property is correlated with reported cash income it follows that the gap between rich and poor is far greater than would appear from the published distributions.

Now the presence — or absence — of this "psychic income" is of crucial importance in determining the attitudes and expectations of the next generation of producers. A child brought up in a prosperous household, surrounded by all the amenities of civilized life, must be exceptionally incompetent and perverse if he fails to secure at least the same level of comfort and culture for himself and his own children. A child born to an indigent family who grows up in noise, squalor, ignorance, and apathy must be uncommonly gifted and industrious to break out of the "poverty cycle" and rise very far beyond the condition of his parents. The exceptions exist. But for most people, not just in Canada now but in all places and at most times, "station in life" is predestinated by family background. The most important ingredient in that background is property. In any society, therefore, in which there is economic freedom to earn an income commensurate with one's contribution to national product, the existence of private property will amplify and make permanent those inequalities which arise from differences in ability, training, and luck.

Now in a rich country like Canada, even the poorest may have a larger real income than an African chief or a medieval baron. But their small relative share, by debarring them from any market influence on the composition of output, leaves them economically powerless. *De facto* political power is dependent on economic power. For this reason it is now customary to define "poverty" in terms of relative, not absolute, income. Hence private property, by perpetuating inequality, is a cause of poverty. It is in this sense, I believe, that it is correct to say that "property is theft."

The Christian View of Property and Theft

Both the Old Testament and the Christian Church acknowledge the injustice of gross inequality. Both see a connexion between private property and undeserved gradations in income and wealth. Yet both uphold a right of individuals and families to own property.

It has been conjectured by German scholars that the eighth commandment originally possessed a direct object ("Thou shalt not steal *men*") and was a prohibition of kidnapping only later extended to material possessions by use of the intransitive form. However this may be, the Old Testament as we now receive it takes for granted the right to own land (Gen 23:4–20; Lev 27:16–25; Nu 26:53–6; Deut 19:14, etc.), wives (Gen 29:19–22; 34:4–12; Ex 20:17), slaves (Gen 37:28; 21:1–11; Lev 25:44–6), houses (Ex 20:17; Lev 29:29–34), cattle

(Gen 13:2; 24:35; etc.), precious metals and money (Gen 24:35; Ex 25:13; Nu 3:48-51), and all manner of personal and household goods. The prophets denounced theft in the same breath as murder, adultery, sacrilege, and perjury (Jer 7:9; Hos 4:2; Zech 5:3). Property rights of others were to be respected, even though they were enemies (Ex 23:4-5), women (Nu 27:1-11), wage-labourers (Deut 24:14), or aliens (Lev 25:47-52). There is no evidence of widespread communal ownership, and little support for Proudhon's attempted exegesis of the Hebrew word *GNB* (= "steal") as meaning to appropriate for oneself out of the common store.

Yet there is no unconditional and inalienable right to property. All good things are a gift of God (1 Ch 29:10-14): the land belongs to him (Lev 25:23) and is given to Israel collectively to be shared (Nu 26:52-6); wives, slaves, and even cattle are to be treated with humanity and respect (Ex 21:7-11, 26-7; Deut 22:13-9; 21:11-4; 25:4). Man is given dominion "over all the earth" (Gen 2:26) in order to use its goods for his needs, but the desire of possessions for their own sake is forbidden by the tenth commandment and is symbolically punished in the wilderness (Ex 16:20). There is, moreover, a clear recognition that under a regime of private property inequality becomes cumulative and hereditary, and therefore unjust. The Year of Jubilee is instituted to provide a "new deal" every two generations by the manumission of all (Hebrew) slaves and the redistribution to its ancestral owners of all alienated rural (but not urban) real estate (Lev 25:8-54).

The primitive Christian Church accepted the authority of the Old Testament and in particular of the "commandments" (Mt 19:17-9) which Jesus came "not . . . to destroy, but to fulfil" (Mt 5:17). The early and short-lived experiment in communal living (Acts 4:32-5) left undisturbed the prohibition of theft (Ro 2:21; Ep. 4:28). St Paul returned the runaway slave Onesimus to his owner Philemon (Philem). Large possessions were seen as a spiritual danger, however (Mt 19:23-6), and the poor as deserving of justice and compassion (Lk 16:19-25). Yet it is clear that the ministry of Jesus envisaged no political remedy for the social injustice of riches and poverty, notwithstanding the attribution to him (Lk 4:18-9) of the Jubilee message (Is 61:1-2). His kingdom is "not of this world" (Jn

18:36); those who wished to make him an earthly ruler in the hope that he would fill empty bellies were warned to "labour not for the meat that perisheth" (Jn 6:15-27).

As Christianity developed from the creed of a Jewish sect to become the official religion of the Roman Empire, the task of conserving and interpreting the faith fell to those we now recognize as the "Fathers." In general they added as little to the biblical tradition as was consistent with the changing social and economic position of the Church. Indeed it is now believed, notwithstanding the opinions of earlier scholars such as Troeltsch, that "there was no essential change in the basic social doctrines of the Fathers" as the Church acquired wealth and power.

The Fathers denied any merely *natural* right to property, and saw clearly that private property led to gross and unjust inequality between rich and poor. But they held that the sinful condition of humanity — a result of the Fall — made property necesary for survival and proper development in a selfish and predatory world. Communal living was revived in the monastic tradition but never again required of all Christians. Those who taught that it ought to be (Ebionites, Montanists, "Apostolics," and others) were repudiated as heretics. Lactantius (c. 310) attacked communism on the grounds that it was unjust to take away one man's property to give it to another; Clement of Alexandria (c. 200) earned the title "Consoler of the Rich" for his denial of the heretics' claims that the rich could not be saved; Theoderetus (c. 435) wrote a reasoned defence of social inequality that anticipated eighteenth century Anglican apologetic. Augustine (c. 420), the greatest and most influential of the Fathers, argued that since private property originated in a sharing by man of God's gifts to the whole human race, its ultimate distribution must rest with the state; but he drew no reformist or socialistic inferences from this. For Augustine, like all the Fathers, was profoundly "other-worldly," thought little of any scheme for social and economic "progress," and would have echoed the words of his fellow-African Tertullian (c. 200): "I have no concern in this life except to depart from it as speedily as possible."

As the ancient world passed away and the Christian Middle Ages succeeded, the greatest thinkers of the West attempted a grand synthesis of all human knowledge, pagan, Hebrew, and Christian. The Fathers' Pauline contempt for this world was judiciously modified by Greek philosophy. This so-called Scholastic tradition reached its highest achievement in the vast and systematic works of Thomas Aquinas (c. 1225–74).

Though Thomas broke new ground in many areas of thought, however, his teaching on property and theft was conservative, biblical, and Augustinian. He claimed that it is natural for man to own goods in common, for the gifts of God are given to the entire human race. But since private possession is necessary for efficiency and order, it is proper for society to "share out" property to families and individuals and to ratify this in law. It is, however, justifiable to take another's goods in case of necessity, and inordinate accumulation of wealth by the rich is robbery of the poor. Yet where a "just" distribution of goods exists (which for Thomas was consistent with a high degree of inequality) it is a breach of charity to steal from others. In effect, Thomas works out on a large scale the implications of the New Testament doctrine that "love worketh no ill to his neighbour: therefore love is the fulfilling of the law" (Ro 13:10; see Lev 19:11–18; Mt 22:35–40; Ro 13:7–10).

So balanced, sane, and deeply scriptural a view was virtually unchallenged at the Reformation, and remains the classic statement of a specifically "Christian" account of property and theft. The communistic sects of the sixteenth and seventeenth centuries, Anabaptists, Hutterites, Levellers, and Fifth Monarchy men, were rejected by Protestant and Catholic alike. The only new ingredient in the mainstream tradition was supplied by the English philosopher, John Locke (1632–1704).

From his theory of knowledge Locke deduced an individualist psychology and ethic based on a new view of the familiar Aristotelian and Thomistic concept of "natural law." A "natural right" to property grows out of the fact that an individual who appropriates some gift of God to his own use "hath mixed his labour with, and joined to it, something that is his own." The idea passed by way of Adam Smith and Ricardo into Karl Marx's "labour theory of value." More mysteriously it also found its way eventually into the encyclical *Rerum*

Novarum of Pope Leo XIII (1891), where for the first time in catholic history an unqualified right to private property was asserted on the basis of natural law.

The twentieth century has seen many variations of emphasis and nuance, but no essential change in the mainstream tradition. The ecumenical Oxford Conference of 1937 reasserted the traditional view of property. The Lambeth Conference of 1948 strongly criticized "Marxian Communism" and counted the right to own property among those fundamental rights which the Church ought to assert and the state protect. The World Council of Churches, despite its occasional use of revolutionary rhetoric, has abstained from condemning private property outright. The pastoral constitution *Gaudiam et Spes* (1966) of the Second Vatican Council quietly buried the protestant innovations of *Rerum Novarum* and reaffirmed the Thomistic account of property, only adding (following *Mater et Magistri* of Pope John XXIII) that private property is necessary in the modern world as a safeguard of political freedom.

The Failure of Secular Ideology

Private property leads to unjust inequality. The Church condemns unjust inequality yet upholds private property. Is there any way out? Christian anarchists both before and since Proudhon have suggested the abolition of property. After all, the Church has always believed that the gifts of God are given to all people. If each produces according to his or her ability and takes according to need, the eighth commandment is rightly understood as a prohibition of personal possessions.

The objection to this, I believe, is that it ignores sin. A "state of nature" with no laws, police, private property, or marriage ties would not be the idyllic paradise imagined by Rousseau and Godwin but, rather, like Hobbes's war of all against all: and the life of Man, solitary, poor, nasty, brutish and short. Those anarchistic members of our own society who pretend to ignore the "oppressive" structures of civilized life — Doukhobors, hippies, Hutterites, professional criminals, and other devotees of the "alternative lifestyle" — are essentially parasitic upon the rest. Without the framework of national defence, protection of property, transport, utilities, and sanitation, their way of life would collapse.

The alternative of state socialism is only slightly less unrealistic, for it too ignores the prevalence and power of human sin. Marxian theorists assure us that the "dictatorship of the proletariat" is but a stage on the way to the eventual withering away of the state. But they cannot explain clearly how the final transition takes place, nor why a stateless, propertyless society would be any more stable than the romantic anarchy they correctly despise. Meanwhile in Russia, Eastern Europe, China, Cuba, and every other socialist republic waste, inefficiency, shortage, and corruption plague the economy, while the most ruthless oppression of the human spirit is routinely committed in the name of the proletariat. For though Marx undoubedtly had a theoretical point in arguing that human consciousness is determined by the mode of production, no one has yet produced a shred of evidence to show that the switch from capitalist to socialist production has any effect on human selfishness, greed, cruelty, and folly.

None of this should be understood to afford any comfort to apologists for the status quo. Capitalism may well be a more efficient way of producing goods and services than any other yet discovered — though a growing concentration of market power, mass unemployment, regional stagnation, and uncontrollable inflation have led many to have their doubts. But an unregulated capitalist society of the kind so eagerly sought by the American New Right is necessarily an unequal and an unfair society. The system is remarkably sensitive in ministering to the needs of those with the purchasing power. But for reasons I have outlined above the distribution of purchasing power is inescapably biassed. A "submerged" fraction of the population, which may be anything from one-fifth (Canada) to four-fifths (Honduras) is doomed to suffer most of the costs of capitalism while enjoying few of its benefits. The fact, therefore, that there is no possible resolution of Proudhon's paradox ought not to blind us to that "theft" which "property" represents.

Liberal-minded Christians in the democratic West, having understood all this, have pinned their hopes on some kind of compromise: "democratic socialism," regulated capitalism, the "mixed economy," or the "welfare state." The Oxford Conference of 1937, for example, correctly declared that "every argument in defence of property rights which is valid for Christian thinking is also an argument for the widest possible distribution of those rights." But then, with the muddle-headedness characteristic of liberal thought, it went on to draw a "clear distinction between various forms of property . . . personal possession for use, such as the home, has behind it a clearer moral justification than property in the means of production."

Now it is evident from the argument of the first section of this chapter that this proposition is incoherent. "Personal possessions for use such as the home" are quite as much "means of production" as fields and tractors. For they condition the attitudes and expectations of the producer and so provide inputs into the productive process of a similar kind to food and education. A society which nationalized industry but left individuals free to accumulate and inherit "personal possessions for use" could still be highly unequal.

The provision of "free" public education, social insurance, health, and recreational services would make little difference. It has been convincingly shown that the middle classes are the principal beneficiaries of the welfare state. The educated and enterprising know how to get the best for their children out of a state school system, make the most intelligent use of public medicine and dentistry, and are the chief consumers of free or subsidized museums, parks, libraries, and symphony concerts. Moreover, by their employment as social workers, administrators, and civil servants, they have a vested interest in a system which gives them power and prestige at the expense of the poor they are supposed to serve.

It must be said finally that attempts to regulate capitalism either by Keynesian monetary and fiscal policy or by redistributive taxation have disappointed most of the hopes held out for them in the early post-war years. Despite the confident assertions of the 1960s, the business cycle has not become obsolete. The rich have shown an unexpected ability to shift the incidence of designedly "progressive" taxation on to the poorer and weaker members of society. The most obvious effect of a more active role for government has been a vast, and highly unpopular, expansion of the public sector, seriously threatening that very productive efficiency which is the chief justification of capitalism.

I conclude that political remedies for inequality, with or without private property, are illusory. No modern "Jubilee," however cunningly devised, can solve the problem. For if the state is powerful enough to enforce redistribution and make it stick, certain other requirements of justice such as political freedom must disappear. But so long as its power is limited in the name of "liberty" or "democracy," the strong will continue to find ways of oppressing the weak.

Those who share my view will be exposed to two temptations, both of which, I believe, ought to be stedfastly resisted.

The first temptation is to find theological justification for poverty and inequality. This was the approach of a distinguished succession of Anglican divines in the eighteenth and early nineteenth centuries from Paley (1743–1805) and Malthus (1766–1834) to Archbishops Whately (1787–1863) and J.B. Sumner (1780–1862). Despite the high intellectual level of their work it must be judged a failure. There is no getting round palpable injustice.

The second temptation is to despair of progress and withdraw from political engagement to a "spiritual" life directed solely to a heavenly existence. This would be wrong for two reasons. In the first place, though Christians ought indeed to be "other worldly," believing that their citizenship is in heaven (Phil 3:20; Heb 13:14), the Church is clearly intended to be the means of extending God's kingdom on earth. And secondly, the fact that there is no comprehensive, ready-made piece of political magic for healing our disordered world does not imply escape from the Christian duty to attack the evils of society and work for reform and improvement. The important thing is to beware of false prophets, knowing that no secular ideology can deal with the root of the matter. For that is buried deep in the primordial corruption of human nature, and only the blood of Christ is physic for that ill.

Note

1   Pierre Joseph Proudhon (1809–65), French socialist whose
    Qu'est-ce que la propriete? (Paris, 1840) influenced Marx
    and is a land-mark in revolutionary thought. Though Pro-
    udhon attacked the Church he was strongly influenced by
    the Bible, and (despite his conventional view of marriage
    and family) his theories were more anarchist than socialist.
    For this reason they were eventually repudiated by Marxist
    communism as "petit bourgeois."

Public Morality and Politics

Gordon Fairweather

9 Thou shalt not bear false witness

Anyone who attempts to take part in a discussion about morality and politics faces the formidable roadblocks of preconceptions and even prejudice. H.L. Mencken wrote of politicians, "It would be hard to find any other class of presumably reputable men who show so high an average of rogues and charlatans."

None can gainsay the existence of "rogues and charlatans" among the thousand or so members of parliament and the provincial and territorial legislatures and assemblies, but they can be measured as rare species in ones or twos rather than a significant number. This chapter will not be an analysis of the obvious immorality involved in breaches of the criminal code by a very few politicians. Theft is theft, fraud is fraud, corruption is corruption, whether or not these crimes are perpetrated by politicians or the public they serve. Integrity cannot be allocated on the basis of role or vocation. I will explore the theme that the gap between politicians and the rest of us is perceived to be much wider than it really is, and that attempting to justify a course of conduct or to explain an excess on the basis that so and so is "just another politician" is as inaccurate as it is dangerous.

During my political career (25 years), I used to be told, "You are too honest to be a politician." This damning with faint praise never ceased to upset me, because I continue to believe that politics is a noble profession involving, as it must, the whole range of human experience. I used to protest such false flattery by suggesting that there cannot be variations of morality which depend on what ones does in life.

The late Walter Lippman used to fill many of his columns with eloquent claims of the virtues of democracy. The opening sentence in his first book *A Preface to Politics*, written in 1913, will serve to measure the thesis of this chapter.

> Politics does not exist for the sake of demonstrating the superior righteousness of anybody. It is not a competition in deportment. In fact, before you can begin to think about politics at all, you have to abandon the notion that there is a war between good men and bad men. That is one of the great . . . superstitions.

Sources of our Discontent

Having entered a disclaimer about what politics is or is thought to be, perhaps we should reflect about the origin of some of our discontent. There are among us those who offer instant solutions and instant gratification. Modern times have brought us not only instant coffee and powdered soup, but also latter-day medicine men offering nostrums for solving the problems of our times. These pedlars thrive on what might be called nostalgic politics and a growing sense of loss of community and of neighbourhood. People's disappointments and fears are pandered to by those who stress the absolute. Take this strong dose and your troubles will disappear. What valium is to secular anxiety, what fundamentalism is to alienated Christians, doctrinaire solutions are to social problems.

The age in which we live is one of increasing uncertainties, and I cannot believe these uncertainties will lessen in the decade ahead. The threat of nuclear annihilation and a collapse of trust in the ability of science and technology to provide a decent future, for example, trouble school children and adults alike. Such erosion of certainties can lead to cynicism. We are in an age "where only uncertainties are fixed," says Gary Trudeau of the Doonesbury cartoon strip, "when taking a stand has come to mean choosing which trapdoor will stand the weight of your convictions longest. We have overlooked the principles of an earlier age, that reputations be built on moral precepts.''

We should guard against substituting cynicism for principle. By ruling out cynicism, one does not deny our democratic right and responsibility to scrutinize and to question public policy and public people. Of course, some of us will continue to be skeptical, some uncertain, and some impatient. These are not necessarily negative values.

The skepticism of which I write is not negative rejection of the system or the kind where doubting is elevated into a philosophy; rather, it is an ongoing search for truth. The uncertainty I would like you to think about is surely understandable because we citizens do get such a variety of signals from our leaders, which make it difficult for our personal radar screens to sort out the good from the nonsensical. Neither is impatience to be shunned. So much remains to be done so that the weak and the powerless among us can have an equal opportunity to share the bounty of the earth.

Skepticism, uncertainty, and impatience can test the great virtue of democracy by dragging the realities into light, summoning our rulers to declare themselves and to submit to judgement. It is here that the tests of public morality are passed or failed. It is here that humbug is seen for what it is, and manipulation is unmasked as an inadequate technique for enlisting public understanding and support.

"Most of us," as Sandra Gwynn wrote recently in *Saturday Night*, "would like to believe, but are too shy and wary to say [so] out loud." She was referring to F.R. Scott's preface to his *Essays on the Constitution*.

> Changing a constitution confronts a society with the most important choices, for in the constitution will be found the philosophical principles and rules which largely determine the relations of the individual and cultural groups to one another and to the state. If human rights and harmonious relations between cultures are forms of the beautiful, then the state is a work of art that is never finished.

I have thought a good deal about Mrs Gwynn's confession

that many of us are too shy and wary to use words like "beautiful" to describe human rights and harmonious relations, and "work of art" as a way of referring to the state. I must say I agree with her, and cite the example of Robert Mugabe, Prime Minister of Zimbabwe, who reminded his countrymen black and white that, "if yesterday you hated me, today you cannot avoid the love that binds you to me and me to you . . ."

Many Canadians are aware that F.R. Scott is a distinguished poet, as well as being a highly respected constitutional lawyer (and I purposely ranked the word poet before constitutional lawyer). Perhaps the human condition would be improved if there were more poets and fewer lawyers as players. Robert Mugabe presents a different perspective, for we had become inured against hearing words like love and forgiveness from the mouth of one who came from jail and exile to lead a free and independent government. Is our public morality in such a precarious state that we hide from eternal verities? Is the great test of honour contained in the lovely language of Paul's letters to his friends in such disrepute that it is in danger of being abandoned in our time? "And now, my friends, all that is true, all that is noble, all that is just and pure, all that is lovable and gracious, whatever is excellent and admirable — fill your thoughts with these things . . . . then the God of Peace will be with you" (Philippians 4:8,9).

The Dangers of Fundamentalism

The fundamentalists are wrong because they hide behind literalism and ignore the social context in which people live. And it is here that I believe Anglicans must judge themselves and their representatives. If this decade is destined to be marked by the holding to ransom of politicians by groups like the Moral Majority in the United States and Renaissance in Canada, then the public morality is in grave danger. Balance and the ability to compromise are dismissed as being signs of weakness by those whose authoritarian tendencies should disquieten us all. The polity of the West (by which I mean the process of civil government or of ordered society) takes equality as its central principle. Representative parliaments or congresses are the delivery systems for this principle. Yet, if those who represent us in these various assemblies, confronted by a veritable host of complicated issues and options, are to be approved by a solitary litmus test of fundamentalism, then woe betide us all, for we will have reverted to the absolutism of the Inquisition!

Paradoxically, we live at a time in which the infidel Gallileo may be rehabilitated, yet courageous contemporary prophets are being indicted by mean-spirited self-proclaimed judges. Some people are alarmed, and resent the crude tactics used by those who measure worth by a single test or inadequately comprehend the range of issues faced by a politician. The essential reconciling role of political parties and parliaments has been lost sight of as narrow self-interest smothers a wider responsibility. Some turn their backs on the process in frustration and despair. Others profess to hate politics. But the truth is that people cannot secure their freedom and happiness without politics, and those who turn away from politics turn away from life.

Morals and Ethics

It is not going to be any easier in the 1980s to keep a clear head and make the kinds of choices and trade-offs that are essential to our survival. This chapter is not intended to be a polemic, nor should it be partisan, yet I am exhilarated by the prospect of seeking a way through the maze of conflicting interests. I believe that most people can make the difficult decisions that are part and parcel of democratic government. Morality is the rules of conduct of a people; therefore, the governors owe it to the governed to share the information upon which choices will be based. Part of the explanation for public cynicism and despair about government and politicians can be traced to a lack of frankness and openness.

I do not claim to know, for example, whether a proposed dam which is designed to harness the tides of the Bay of Fundy can be justified on the basis of cost-benefit. I do know because of my own curiosity, that to build the dam at the site proposed will mean the destruction of the nesting ground for the largest flock of sandpipers on the eastern flyway of our hemisphere.

This, in itself, does not automatically rule out the building of the dam, but surely the public must be made aware of the consequences of the construction. Perhaps there is no way to reconcile the benefits of a renewable source of electricity with the irretrievable loss of a species of bird-life. Yet the decision should only be made if citizens are informed of the risks.

Another criterion by which the morality of a government can be judged is the quality of its transactions with other states. In this regard, the inevitable conflict between self-interest and disinterestedness, between pragmatism and abstract values, is at the basis of the founding charter of the United Nations. We have heard the pragmatist's side of the argument to an unusual degree in Canada recently as various of our international transactions have been exposed as being subject to questioning. The reactions of many of us have been confused and ambiguous. Some had thought of Canada as one of the most principled of nations, "not like the others," but now we have our doubts.

Professor John Holmes uses the term "enlightened internationalism," and I find the expression apt. An element for me in enlightened internationalism is the acceptance by Canada of moral responsibility for our actions. I do not agree with those who argue that the so-called real world is an unprincipled place and that, to get along in this real world, Canadians should tolerate unprincipled behaviour on the part of their representatives.

The idea that we must accept and even adopt cynical practices and standards in setting the public morality of the state is unacceptable. We would never borrow shoddy standards from another state in determining how we should treat our own citizens in our internal affairs. Why should we adopt the ethical standards of others in, for example, international trade? We *can* make the rules, for our own conduct at least. In my view, we must have principles and stick to them, and the devil take the hindmost.

To paraphrase the late Professor Gordon W. Allport of Harvard, one of the more influential social psychologists of our time, who did extensive research on the nature of prejudice: "If we live for our religion and its total creed (including love for our neighbour), certain things are knit into the fabric of our personalities. Human-heartedness is for us as essential as our belief in God.''

As the Reverend J.A. Davidson wrote recently, ''Deep faith and commitment, entailing regular practice of the religious devotions and disciplines, helps us manage our prejudices; shallow faith and commitment, with only casual practice of the devotions and disciplines, is likely to nourish our prejudices.''

Perhaps by now my biases are becoming evident: that morality and ethics are more than merely staying out of trouble, more than never doing anything that is proscribed by the criminal code. The two words morals and ethics used to be synonymous, now their usage has become divided. There is a growing tendency to limit the use of *immoral* to certain sexual activities while other misdemeanours are described as unethical. My dictionary does not recognize this distinction, neither does my faith accept different codes depending upon one's vocation. In the field of ethics and morals, or right and wrong, there can be no grey areas. An action is either moral or it is not. And I have said, an action can be immoral without being illegal; e.g., if I use information gained by reason of my public office for personal profit or for the benefit of friends or relatives, I may not be guilty of a criminal act, but my action is clearly immoral. It is my thesis that a code of morality does not expand or contract like an accordian depending upon who it is applied to. Obviously a politician is very much a public person, and therefore, his or her transgressions are subject to public scrutiny and comment; yet this fact does not change the dimensions of the code itself.

Having said that about ethics and morals, I will end with a plea not to add to our country's problems by polarizing our society between those who hold religious beliefs and those who do not. We Anglicans are asked if we ''will strive for justice, peace, and human dignity among all peoples and all nations.'' The invitation is not designed to exclude but to reconcile. It is a bidding to love and to understanding of the non-religious people who share most of our goals. In this decade, it will be more important than ever for believers to bear the burden of showing that religious belief and compassionate social action are not antithetical. Religion for me is one source of good morals, and it is a powerful one, but it is not the only one. There are other sources.

Faith, patience, and balance — these are some of the ethical elements of citizenship in these days. An essential quality of the Christian religion is that it be able to respond deeply to human need and not affront humanity. A fair test of people in high office is not how they respond to a particular issue, but rather whether or not they realize the force of moral conviction. They are the custodians of the nation's ideals, of the hopes and faith that sustains Canada from one generation to another. We are, in the final analysis, all involved in the pain of the world.

Coveting amid Affluence

John Bothwell

10   Thou shalt not covet

"Well now, that's better — but it's still not good enough!" This exclamation came from a piano teacher. For even though young Tommy had hit all the proper notes of the popular tune he was practising, without even a single discord, no one was likely to start singing or dancing in response to his kind of music. The spirit simply wasn't there! So the teacher insisted on something more.

Well, many modern people feel that way about the Ten Commandments too. Like Tommy's music, the commandments strike some important notes, but they seem to lack warmth and spirit. Thus words like "Thou shalt not covet —" seem unlikely to "turn on" many people any more. Indeed, some younger folk hardly understand what *covet* means. A seventeen year old, from a good church family, assured me recently that she had never even heard of the word!

But, of course, regular Bible readers have heard of it and have experienced it too. Even so, sometimes its meaning is not really clear. Years ago at Sunday School I was told that *to covet* meant "to want things that you aren't willing to work for." And it was surely no accident that, by this definition, serious-minded middle-class Christians, devoted to the old-fashioned work ethic (i.e. "our kind of people") could hardly be guilty, especially if they were already fairly prosperous.

But that's nonsense, of course! Willingness to work hard toward a better standard of living for one's self or one's children may be very commendable, but it is no guarantee of freedom from covetousness, at least not by biblical standards.

The Meaning of Covet

Well then, clearly and succinctly, what does "Thou shalt not covet" really mean? Coveting does not rule out a normal desire to acquire "good things" either for one's self or for one's family: such a desire is natural and human. Nor does it preclude the wish that we might possess for ourselves the talents or qualities that we admire most in others. In other words, normal human feelings are quite acceptable. But when the fulfilment of our own desires might prove harmful to others, or to ourselves, and yet we still persist in directing our thoughts toward such fulfilment, then that is covetousness.

Biblical scholars assure us that in the original text of Exodus Chapter 20, the Hebrew word for *covet* clearly suggests the idea of indulgence in harmful thoughts. And in the Deuteronomy Chapter 5 version of the commandments, another different Hebrew word emphasizes even more clearly the intention to "prohibit grasping thoughts that lead to grasping deeds."[1] It seems fair to claim, therefore, that grudging discontent which leads to ruthless acquisition is the heart of the biblical view of coveting.

Now if the tenth commandment is an explicit early recognition of the importance of our "inner thoughts and inner life," then in a certain sense it is the most important of all the commandments. For the tenth commandment represents the spirit in which the others are to be understood, the spirit that we so often fail to discern. That warning against coveting clearly foreshadows the warning of our Lord Christ when he said, centuries later, according to St Matthew,

> Listen to me, and understand this: a person is not defiled by what goes into the mouth, but by what comes out of it . . . . What comes out of the mouth has its origins in the heart; and that is what defiles . . . . Wicked thoughts, murder, adultery, fornication, theft, perjury, slander, — these all proceed from the heart; and these are the things that defile.[2]

In sum, the inward emphasis of the tenth commandment delineates, clearly and succinctly, the most potent source of infidelity to the other nine. And in so doing, it points forward to the teachings of Jesus Christ and, at the same time, gives warning to pious legalists that the mere avoidance of killing, stealing, and adultery is not enough. Inner thoughts and attitudes are the heart of the matter of obedience.

The Origin of Evil

We have in the tenth commandment then, a kind of "theology" about the source of evil. Where does evil originate? It is not caused by material things. The biblical creation story in Genesis, with its recurring theme, "and God saw that it was good,"[3] reminds us that physical things have a divine purpose, and should not be despised or rejected.

Further, the use by humans of animals, birds, fish, and indeed the whole earth and its products, is positively affirmed by a biblical faith.[4] In fact, even private property is legitimized in the Bible, but with an important reservation. For according to scripture, God is the Sovereign Lord of all life,[5] and therefore, God alone has absolute property rights. The Old Testament insists that our human right to private property is, in principle, subordinate to the obligation to care for the weaker members of society.[6] And this view is reinforced in the New Testament.[7] According to God's priorities, "The life of each and every individual, even the poorest, is of greater value than all material things."[8]

Therefore, every human being can feel quite free to want and use and enjoy the good things of the world, and even claim ownership for one's self of a fair share of them; but it is essential for Christians to take care to share their bounty, especially with the poor and needy. This is a fair, brief summary of the biblical view. And our clear understanding of its meaning for us, including a willingness to accept the moral imperative of sharing, is surely one of the major issues of faith in our time. For as the noted American theologian Robert McAfee Brown has claimed:

> The problems of faith . . . today are no longer so much academic (the mind/body problem, the relationship of freedom and necessity . . . etc.) — as they are human/social. (Why does faith not empower people to change? How can we contain the forces of evil? . . . . Why are we so reluctant to side with the poor?)
>
> Two different Bibles emerge depending on the perspective from which the one Bible is read. One perspective very skillfully justifies western, bourgeois, capitalist culture.

This is the comforting Bible we have read. The other challenges all the assumptions of that culture, and offers ingredients for creating an alternative world.[9]

Buf if evil does not reside in things, is its source in the temptations we feel from other people? The social sciences have demonstrated convincingly the manner in which our personal ideas and choices can change because of social pressures. In this connection sociologist Peter Berger writes,

> We obtain our notions about the world originally from other human beings, and these notions continue to be plausible to us in a very large measure because others continue to affirm them.[10]

Thus a young Christian leaving home for the first time soon feels tempted to question the validity of the ideas and values of his/her upbringing. It could hardly be otherwise, for the "significant others" in his/her life have changed. And since our Canadian culture is indeed "post-Christian" (i.e. oriented toward success and technology much more than toward Christian values and people), then clearly we Christians have a serious problem. Peter Berger has emphasized, therefore, that modern Christians have no choice but to "huddle together" for mutual support in local Christian counter-culture communities. Only thus can our Christian values be preserved from erosion by the acids of secularism. Social pressure is indeed a serious threat to us, but "Christian community" can provide the antidote.

So evil does not originate in "things," at least not unless we choose selfishly. Nor is it caused necessarily by social pressure, unless we lack or ignore the support of Christian fellowship. Evil does not originate in our own legitimate desires either, as we saw above. What then is its source? Let's face it, the chief source of evil is within us, in our hearts and minds and wills, and covetousness, that "grudging discontent that leads to ruthless acquisition," is one of its chief sources. No wonder Archbishop William Temple regarded "self-centredness and all the welter of evil flowing from it" as the essence of sin.[11]

Covetousness as a Canadian Threat

Well now, we have discussed what it means *to covet*, and demonstrated how the Bible sees covetousness as a prime source of evil. One important question remains: in what sense is covetousness a special threat to us modern Canadians?

In recent years, we have witnessed the rise of wide-spread public suspicion of greed and covetousness in two sectors of society. On the one hand, there is unease about great multi-national corporations, like the oil companies, for example, which, despite their disclaimers, are presumed to make enormous profits, and to be more influential and powerful internationally than all but the most powerful nations. And on the other hand, there is an equal distrust of "welfare bums," that is, of allegedly lazy and indifferent individuals who refuse to do honest work and live at public expense through welfare payments. This latter suspicion is unwarranted and has been demonstrated as such,[12] and unease about large companies may be unwarranted too, although suspicion still persists. The popular public presumption seems to be that if we could only control greedy corporations and irresponsible welfare recipients, then society as a whole would be immeasurably better off. Because most of us, it is assumed, are really pretty decent folk.

Decent we may be, but while average Canadians are among the most affluent citizens on earth, there is no evidence to suggest either that we are content with our lot or that we are generous with our substance. A social scientist with a flair for statistics estimated that while fifty years ago our grandparents regarded about forty different items as the "essentials of life," today most of us consider nearly two hundred items as such, including articles like television sets — with colour!

In a similar vein, but more concretely, from 1970 to 1977 we are assured that "the net worth of Canadian households, (families and people living alone) increased about 150% (income rose 100%), and personal savings tripled to become the highest in the world, while prices went up only 65%."[13] But during the same period (1970 to 1977), the percentage of Canadian tax-payers claiming the automatic hundred dollar tax deduction for medical expenses and charitable gifts combined (instead of submitting receipts as evidence of more generous charitable gifts) increased from just over 70% to 90%. And even among faithful church folk, "the average giving of confirmed Anglicans in 1977 lingered at only $108.00 a year, during the same year that the average annual household income was $19,850."[14]

As our society becomes more affluent then, Canadians with rising personal expectations apparently have become less generous. Could this be labelled *covetousness*? Surely it can; but if not, then what could it be called? The plain unpalatable truth seems to be that both our corporate social conduct and our selfish individual habits are rooted in insensitive selfishness.

In his impressive paperback entitled *Rich Christians in a Hungry World*, Dr Ronald Sider compares the modern world to a very long railway train in which a few privileged passengers (chiefly those of us who live in the "developed nations" like Canada) ride first-class, in conditions of incredible comfort, while the overwhelming majority is crammed into livestock cars that make up most of the train. Dr Sider asks,

> Do Christians today have the kind of faith and courage that will pioneer new models of sharing with the world's starving millions?

And then, answering his own question, he comments,

> Sadly, I must confess my fear that the majority of affluent Christians of all theological labels have bowed the knee to Mammon. If forced to choose between defending their luxuries and following Jesus amongst the oppressed, I am afraid they will imitate the rich young ruler.[15]

In a similar spirit, Dom Helder Camara, the famous Brazilian Roman Catholic archbishop who has devoted his life to seeking justice for the poor, writes,

> I used to think when I was a child that Christ was exaggerating when He warned about the dangers of wealth. Today, I know better. I know how very hard it is to be rich, and still keep the milk of human-kindness. Money has a dangerous way of putting scales on one's eyes, and a dangerous way of freezing people's hands, eyes, lips, and hearts.[16]

Or yet again, in the words of the New Testament's First Epistle to St Timothy,

> Those who want to get rich fall into temptation and are caught in the trap of many foolish and harmful desires, which pull them down to ruin and destruction. For the love of money is the source of all kinds of evil. Some have been so eager to have it that they have wandered away from the faith. [17]

Obviously, the temptation to insensitivity towards others' needs, *covetousness*, that arises from belonging to the affluent minority in a hungry world, requires far more from us than merely donating a few more dollars to the Primate's World Relief and Development Fund, even though such generosity in itself would be commendable. Something more is required, particularly when we consider such "structural social evils" as —

> our squandering of disappearing non-renewable energy and mineral resources,

> our economic and trading exploitation of underdeveloped countries (including our unwillingness to treat the United Nations' "new international economic order" seriously),

> our addiction to beefsteak, which leads us to feed even more grain protein to our beef cattle, while citizens of the Third-World countries do without protein,

> our insensitivity to the wants and needs of our own native Canadian Indian and Eskimo.

Clearly, massive changes in our attitudes and life-style are called for corporately as well as individually. A careful study of the statistics of some of these issues, in Dr Sider's book or elsewhere, will make this abundantly clear. The fact is that affluent Canadian Christians need to repent, both for our own sakes and on behalf of all Canadians. For *covetousness*, that "grudging discontent that leads to ruthless acquisition," seems to hold us firmly in its greedy grasp. And Christians, who are schooled in the biblical notion of *repentance (metanoia)*, will understand that the word means literally "turning around," having a total change of mind. Without doubt, that's what we need with regard to our personal habits and life-style!

Encouraged by constant seductive advertising, intimidated by fear of galloping inflation, and convinced that we deserve parity, at the very least, with the more affluent "Jones" in the next block, we Canadians buy lottery tickets in record amounts, and often turn a deaf ear when charities come begging.

Dr Sider suggests we take Zacchaeus as our model.[18] As a greedy tax-collector for the Roman Empire, Zacchaeus was enmeshed in sinful economic structures and personal exploitation of others. But when he came to Jesus, he knew that his personal habits and life-style would have to change. What a similar kind of repentance might mean for many of us is disturbing, indeed frightening, to contemplate. But then the ultimate consequences in terms of divine judgment, if we do not change, is even more frightening. Please read Chapter 25 of St Matthew's Gospel for further details!

Wealth and Deprivation

During the summer of 1980 *Time* magazine featured an article about urban renewal on Manhatten Island, New York. It spoke encouragingly about new building projects and cultural renewal, and claimed that Manhatten is "beautiful, rich, and piled high with roof gardens that give shade to some very rich and beautiful people." But it also commented on the hopeless slums. "The businessmen and politicians are always putting up new buildings downtown, and talking about how good things in New York are getting," commented a South Bronx housewife, "but they haven't been up here!" It's a tale of two cities, "the best of times and the worst." One prominent New Yorker summed it up by saying, "What we have in the city right now is an island on which enormous wealth is being created, surrounded by a sea of economic deprivation."[19]

Let New York City (or Montreal, Toronto, or Vancouver) serve as a symbol, a microcosm of the whole world. "Enormous wealth — surrounded by deprivation." That's the way things are in the whole world today. We who are middle-class Canadian Christians may not think of ourselves as wealthy, but in fact we are among the most fortunate and wealthy people who have ever lived on this planet earth. Therefore, we have a special need to "beware of covetousness." For "grudging discontent leads to ruthless acquisition," and both parts of this definition seem characteristic of our Canadian way of life!

Notes

1 *Interpreter's Bible*, Volume 1, p. 989.

2 Matthew 15:10, 11, 19, 20.

3 Genesis 1.

4 Genesis 1:26.

5 Job 41:11, Psalm 50:12, Exodus 19:5.

6 M. Hengel, *Property and Riches in the Early Church*, (Philadelphia: Fortress, 1975) p. 12.

7 St Luke 12:33–34, 1 Timothy 6:17–18, Hebrew 13:5.

8 See *Biblical Authority Today*, ed. by Alan Richardson and W. Schweitzer (London: SCM Press, 1951), p. 261.

9 R.M. Brown "Starting Over: New Beginning Points for Theology," *The Christian Century*, 14 May 1980.

10 Peter Berger, *A Rumour of Angels*, (Garden City: Doubleday, 1968), p. 17.

11 Joseph Fletcher, *William Temple, Twentieth Century Saint*, (Geneva: Allenson, 1963).

12 See *Beyond Stereotypes*, A Report of the Hamilton Social Planning and Research Council, 1976.

13 See Report to General Synod, *Sent in Mission Beyond Ourselves*, June 1980.

14 Ibid.

15 Ronald J. Sider, *Rich Christians in a Hungry World*, (Downers Grove: Inter Varsity Press, 1977).

16 H. Camara, *Revolution Through Peace*, (New York: Harper-Row, 1971).

17 1 Timothy 6:9, 10.

18 See Luke 19:1–10.

19 *Time Magazine*, 18 August 1980.